Proslogion

St. Anselm of Canterbury

Proslogion

Including Gaunilo's Objections and Anselm's Reply

Translated and Introduced by Matthew D. Walz

St. Augustine's Press
South Bend, Indiana

Manufactured in the United States of America

2 3 4 5 6   26 25 24 23 22 21 20

Library of Congress Cataloging in Publication Data
Anselm, Saint, Archbishop of Canterbury, 1033–1109.
[Proslogion. English]
Proslogion: including Gaunilo's objections and Anselm's reply /
St. Anselm of Canterbury;
translated and introduced by Matthew D. Walz. – 1st [edition].
pages   cm
Includes bibliographical references and index.
ISBN 978-1-58731-659-3 (paperbound : alk. paper) –
ISBN 978-1-58731-660-9 (e-book)
1. God – Proof, Ontological – Early works to 1800.
I. Walz, Matthew D., translator, writer of added commentary.
II. Gaunilo, 11th cent. Liber pro insipiente. English. III. Anselm, Saint,
Archbishop of Canterbury, 1033–1109. Liber apologeticus. English.
IV. Title.
B765.A83P7613 2013
212'.1 – dc23   2012039820

∞The paper used in this publication meets the minimum requirements of
the American National Standard for Information Sciences Permanence of
Paper for Printed Materials, ANSI Z39.481984.

ST AUGUSTINE'S PRESS
www.staugustine.net

Sponsae formosae meae et matri filiorum nostrorum amanti,
TERESIAE

. . . quoniam caritas ex Deo est . . .

Introduction

In 593 AD, Pope Gregory the Great wrote the *Dialogues*. This work comprises four books recounting conversations between Gregory and a young man named Peter concerning "the life and miracles of the Italian Fathers." The aim of the *Dialogues*, it appears, is to instill hope in Christians by providing models of the spiritual life. In other words, by means of examples, the work argues that holiness is truly possible in this life. In three of the four books, lives of numerous Italian Fathers are recorded; Gregory honors only one Italian Father with an entire book dedicated to recording his life and miracles. That man, of course, is Benedict of Nursia – or "the man of God" (*vir Dei*), as Gregory often names him. It is a fitting tribute to a man who, by his life and only a single written work, the *Rule*, shaped Western monasticism and by extension the development of Europe as a whole. To Gregory, who himself lived as a monk under the *Rule* prior to becoming the pope, Benedict stands out as a sign of hope in a world in need of Christian exemplars.

Medieval monks in the West, among whom Anselm of Canterbury is counted, studied Benedict's *Rule*. More than likely they also read Gregory's account of Benedict's life in the *Dialogues*. They would have pondered, then, a marvelous event that took place near the end of Benedict's marvel-filled life. Gregory recounts it thus:

> While the monks were still resting, the man of God, Benedict, who was constant in keeping watch, rose up before the time of night prayer. Standing at the window and praying to the all-able God, and looking out at the hour of darkest night, he suddenly saw light being poured out from above, which made all the darkness of night flee and became bright with much splendor, so much so that this light radiating in the midst of the darkness would have overcome day itself. During this spectacular sight, moreover, an exceedingly wonderful thing followed, which Benedict himself told afterward: the whole world, gathered together as if under a single ray of the sun, was brought together before his eyes.[1]

As Gregory points out, it was Benedict himself, a man of great humility throughout his life, who related this event to others. Presumably the man of God considered it an event worth telling.

What are we to make of this event? The world, which *prima facie* strikes us as greater than ourselves, appears small and comprehensible to the eyes and understanding of the man of God. As the *Dialogues* indicate, Gregory and Peter are amazed by this story, and Gregory attempts to unfold its significance to his young interlocutor. He says:

> Hold firm, Peter, to what I say, because to the soul that sees the Creator, every creature is narrow. For no matter how slightly the soul looks forth from the light of the Creator, all that is created becomes little to it. This is because the bosom of the mind is opened up by the very light of its inmost vision and is expanded in God, in such a way that it exists as higher than the world; indeed, the very soul of the one seeing is also above itself. Since it is thus caught up above itself in the light of God, it is amplified in its interior. Thus lifted up, when it looks upon itself below itself, it comprehends how little it is able to comprehend when it is lowered. . . . What wonder is it, then, that the man of God saw the world gathered together before himself, who in the light of his mind was elevated outside the world? And although the world was gathered together before his eyes, yet heaven and earth were not contracted; rather, the soul of the one seeing is widened, who, caught up in God, can see without difficulty all that is under God.[2]

Thus was Benedict, "blessed [*benedictus*] both by grace and by name,"[3] blessed by this unique vision in which were revealed both the greatness of God the Creator and the smallness of the world He created.

Why begin an introduction to Anselm's *Proslogion* by recounting a marvelous event from the life of Benedict? Indeed, these two events – Benedict's vision and the publication of the *Proslogion* – stand nearly half of a millennium apart. One reason is to call attention to the fact that even by his own account Anselm was first and foremost a Benedictine monk, a vocation and state that defined him as a person and a thinker. Anselm was a monastic, not a scholastic, even though the *Proslogion* is often read as if Anselm should be numbered among the Schoolmen. Now, it would carry us too far afield here to spell out the relevant distinctions between monasticism and scholasticism.[4] For the sake of this introduction, it suffices to note that Anselm's intellectual life in the monastery (before becoming a bishop) was essentially communal; hence, what he wrote was intended chiefly for the intellectual and spiritual benefit of his brethren. He was not, therefore, a "professional theologian" who lectured at a city university, but a monk who conversed daily with his brethren about divine matters. To understand the *Proslogion*, then, it behooves us to acknowledge Anselm's purpose in writing it as well as the intellectual and spiritual climate within which it came to birth.

Another, more specific reason I begin with a story from Benedict's life is to suggest a reading of the *Proslogion* that looks forward from Benedict to Anselm rather than backward from Kant or Descartes (or even Aquinas) to

Anselm. Perhaps more than any other work in the history of philosophy, the *Proslogion* has become encrusted with layers of (mis)interpretation. Most recent interpreters operate under the assumption that Anselm was the first proponent of what Kant first termed an "ontological argument" for God's existence. Interpretations along these lines even depict Anselm's argument in the *Proslogion* – usually identified only with Chapters 2, 3, and 4 – in the "language" of symbolic logic, modal operators, and the like. Ripping these chapters untimely from the womb of the *Proslogion*, however, issues in abortive accounts of Anselm's thinking. But if one reads the work looking forward from Benedict, one is less likely to analyze the *Proslogion* according to the presuppositions of modern philosophy or scholasticism and more likely to see it as a concise synthesis of an intelligently focused monastic worldview that bears fruit in insights into the reality of God. Indeed, as I would like to suggest, the *Proslogion* derives from and accords with the sort of experience that Benedict had while keeping vigil at his window late that night as his brethren slept, an experience that derives from a perspective on human existence and the existence of the world attained by one dedicated to an ascetic manner of living, i.e., a life of physical, moral, intellectual, and spiritual "self-pruning." And even if we readers are unlikely to enter into Anselm's asceticism, we must be willing at least to give ourselves over to keeping constant watch with him as he thinks the reality of God in the *Proslogion*. Anselm has crafted this work with great care, and he invites his reader to experience what he himself experienced with regard to God within the liberating confines of his monastic existence.

There is, finally, a third reason why I draw attention to Benedict's vision here, namely, to suggest a particular manner of reading the *Proslogion*. As Anselm indicates in its Preface, this work recapitulates an intellectual (perhaps even mystical) experience that he himself underwent. This experience culminated in the reception of a "thought," a *cogitatio*, which Anselm first articulates in Chapter 2 as *aliquid quo nihil maius cogitari possit* ("something than which nothing greater is able to be thought"), the *Proslogion*'s best-known but oft-misunderstood phrase. By recalling Benedict's miraculous vision, I want to suggest that the thought that "offered itself" to Anselm in a moment of despair is comparable to the sun's ray along which Benedict gazed upon the entire world – even if Anselm gazed along that ray from the opposite end. By means of that ray of the sun, Benedict beheld in a moment the whole world's beauty gathered together within a single divine-like gaze, and at the same time (as Gregory points out) he grasped the narrowness and smallness of that world inasmuch as it is not the Uncreated but created. It is helpful for appreciating the *Proslogion*, I think, to consider Anselm's unique thought as a ray of the sun along which he gazes upward from the world to the God who dwells in unapproachable light, and we readers are invited to gaze along this ray with him.

This approach to God demands attaining a new perspective on the world, which entails the amplification of the mind's eye so as to come closer to the Creator's vision of all that is. The *Proslogion* permits this; it allows us to enter into Anselm's *cogitatio*, his very activity of thinking something than which nothing greater is able to be thought, so that with him we may unveil and unfold the necessity and truth of the divine existence that stands as the ever-elusive extremity of human thinking as well as the very ground of the world's thinkability.

To be sure, Benedict's vision is not the only notable precedent analogous to what Anselm recapitulates in the *Proslogion*. Another is the vision at Ostia that Augustine shares with Monica, which Augustine spends the bulk of Book X of the *Confessions* spelling out in accordance with the mind's step-by-step ascent to God. Indeed, as a dedicated follower of Augustine, Anselm may have had in mind this event as well as Benedict's vision when he wrote the *Proslogion*; there are, in fact, resonances of both in various words, phrases, and images in Anselm's text. Whatever connections there be, though, I hope the chief point is clear: Anselm's *Proslogion* is best understood as an invitation to share in a unique *cogitatio*, a singular activity of thinking the reality of God with which Anselm was blessed and which he hopes to share with us readers. Unless we readers enter into this thinking with him, and thereby avoid the temptation of reducing the argument of the *Proslogion* to a discourse express-ible in syllogisms or symbolic logic, we simply will not be engaging with this work in the manner in which its author intended.

Anselm of Bec, author of the *Proslogion*

In 1059, at the age of twenty-seven, a young man named Anselm arrived at the Benedictine abbey in Bec, France, apparently in search of an education. By a wandering path, he had made his way from Aosta, a mountainous region in northern Italy. The roundabout journey, it appears, had taken four years. We know little of what took place during that time and, indeed, during Anselm's childhood. Afterwards, Anselm himself spoke little about his life prior to arriving at Bec. We can gather that his mother died before his departure from Aosta and that there was a falling-out with his father. It is likely, moreover, that he came to Bec primarily in order to study under its abbot, Lanfranc, who had earned a wide reputation as a teacher of letters. We may surmise as well that he came not only to be educated, but also to find a new home, because in 1060, Anselm decided to become a monk of the abbey. He progressed within in the community quickly; in 1063, he was made prior, and in 1078, abbot. He remained at Bec until 1093, when he was appointed Archbishop of Canterbury, an office he was none too eager to take up. Until his death in 1109, Anselm's life was busy – too busy for his taste. The details of his last sixteen years an interested reader can discover elsewhere.[5] Here it is fitting to reflect briefly on Anselm's early years at Bec around the time he wrote the *Proslogion*.

Although we do not know exact dates, the *Proslogion* was likely completed around 1077/78. It was the third work Anselm published. The first was an oft-neglected dialogue called *De grammatico* (*On the Grammarian*), likely completed between 1060 and 1063, not long after Anselm settled in at the monastery. On the surface this dialogue explores denominative or paronymous naming, an issue treated briefly by Aristotle in Chapter 1 of his *Categories*. Under the surface, though, Anselm is exploring the intricacies of the relationship between grammar and logic, no small matter for a man of letters during this transitional period in Western medieval history. Around this same time, moreover, Anselm was penning prayers and meditations, many of which were gathered into collections at a later date.

About fifteen years passed before Anselm's next major work was published. The *Monologion* was completed around 1075/76. In its Prologue, Anselm indicates that he wrote it at the behest of his brother monks with a view to providing a model for meditating on the divine essence. No doubt his brethren were inspired by Anselm, who shone as a teacher and guide during their ongoing monastic conversations concerning divine matters. According to Anselm, these monks insisted that he not make use of Scriptural authority in the *Monologion*, but rather that he reach his conclusions through the "necessity of reason" (about which I will say more below). After its initial publication, the *Monologion* began to be copied widely; Anselm himself, however, was dissatisfied. As he reveals in the Preface of the *Proslogion*, which he published just a year or two later around 1078/79, Anselm considered the *Monologion* a work "interwoven by the chaining together of many arguments." In fact, his desire to unify the chain of reasoning in the *Monologion* led him to the brink of intellectual despair, since he seemed incapable of laying hold of *unum argumentum*, a single argument or line of reasoning that would encapsulate his meditation on the divine essence.

The *Proslogion* came to birth, then, in a moment of despair. In his *Life of Anselm*, Anselm's student and friend Eadmer reports on what took place after the publication of the *Monologion*, an account that confirms and expands on what Anselm tells us in the Preface of the *Proslogion*:

> After these things [i.e., the publication of the *Monologion* and its aftermath] it came into his mind to investigate whether what is believed and said about God would be able to be proved by only a single brief argument, namely, that he is eternal, unchangeable, all-able, everywhere as a whole, incomprehensible, just, kind, pity-hearted, true, truth, goodness, justice, and other such things, and in what manner these are one in him. This very thing, as he himself indicated, gave birth to a great hardship for

him. For, on the one hand, this thought took him away from food, drink, and sleep; and, on the other hand, it disturbed the attention that he ought to have paid to morning prayer and the other service of God – and this latter consequence weighed on him more. Attending to this fact, and yet still not capable of grasping fully what he was seeking, he judged that this thought was a temptation of the devil, and he decided to push it far away from his attention. Yet, in truth, to the extent that he exerted himself in doing so, to that same extent this very thought harassed him more and more. And, behold, on a certain night, between the night watches, the grace of God shone in his heart, and the reality made itself clear to his understanding, and it filled his inmost self with unmeasured joy and jubilation. Deeming, therefore, that this very thing that happened to him would be able to please others as well, without envy he immediately wrote it on tablets, and he gave them to one of the brothers from the monastery to guard them.[6]

The *Proslogion*, then, is Anselm's attempt to recapitulate this intellectual and spiritual event. As Anselm relates it in the Preface, "[I]n this very conflict of thoughts that of which I had despaired offered itself in such a way that I eagerly embraced the thought [*cogitationem*] that in my troubled state I had been pushing away." It is a thought, I would suggest, that makes the truth and reality of God's existence present to human intelligence – that is, if the reader willingly, openly, and strenuously endeavors to think "something than which nothing greater is able to be thought."

As an author, then, Anselm's intention in writing the *Proslogion* is to share the gift of this thought and to unfold its intelligibility. Why? So that the reader, too, may be pleased with this gift just as Anselm himself was. In carrying out this task, Anselm wrote "under the person [*sub persona*] of one endeavoring to straighten up his mind toward contemplating God and seeking to understand what he believes," as he tells us in the Preface. If we are to read this work well, then, we must take on this same *persona* and make it our own, thereby attempting to align our thinking with the thinking of Anselm, who is striving to align his thinking with the very reality of God to which he faithfully assents.

What the *Proslogion* is about

The *Proslogion* is about God. What could be clearer than that? Yet we need to be nuanced on this score, since human thinking is not really able to be *about* God, since this would suggest a stance of human intelligence "over against" God, as if God were able to be an "object" before the mind's eye. If this were the case, as Anselm ably puts it in Chapter 4, "a creature would ascend above the Creator and would judge about the Creator – which is very absurd." It may be more accurate, then, to say that the *Proslogion* is about the activity of think-ing God as much as one is able in this life. It depicts in writing the activity of thinking God so as to make the reality of God manifest in that very activity. But such an activity never stops, never finds rest; indeed, it is unable to come to a rest, at least in this life. The *Proslogion*, then, depicts Anselm's relentless intellectual pursuit of God, which stems from a restless heart desirous of God. It is an essentially zetetic work.

Anselm's original title of the *Proslogion* indicates as much. It was first entitled *Fides quaerens intellectum*, i.e., *Faith Seeking Understanding* – or, perhaps, *Trust Striving after Insight*. We should be grateful that Anselm reveals this original title in the Preface, as it encapsulates the character of the work. After Anselm awakens the reader to the image of God dwelling within himself in Chapter 1, he begins Chapter 2 with an act of faith or trust, namely, his assent to the proposal of God as "something than which nothing greater is able to be thought." For, in accord with Augustine, Anselm knows that to believe (*credere*) is to think with assent (*cogitare cum assensu*). But this proposal, this thought of God as "something than which nothing greater is able to be thought," begs to be understood; it draws us into itself by its hidden intelligi-bility. In the remainder of the work, therefore, Anselm endeavors to think-with-assent "something than which nothing greater is able to be thought" (*fides*) in order to unfold spiritedly its significance (*quaerens*) and to arrive thereby at a deeper and more adequate insight into the reality it signifies (*intel-lectum*).

In this thought of God offered to him in his despair, Anselm discovers with delight that it begins to align the very activity of his thinking with the purely active, overflowing, creative reality of God. In other words, thinking through this thought and striving to understand what it signifies stretches one toward apprehending the divine reality as both so true that it is not able to be thought not to be and so good that it is freely diffusive of being and truth, yet in such a way that that divine reality remains undiminished in its ever-greater-ness. This is because thinking "something than which nothing greater is able to be thought" at once unveils the manifest character of the divine reality (if there is going to be any thinking at all) and yet never allows that activity of thinking to come to a rest (because the thought is not of some determinate and intelligible reality, but always points beyond such realities toward the abyss of intelligibility that is their source).

Allow me to suggest, then, that the *Proslogion* is about God obliquely; more directly it concerns the activity of thinking God. Indeed, it *depicts* that activity. The *Proslogion* depicts *fides quaerens intellectum*, trust striving after insight into the reality of God. Here I can only suggest such a reading; argu-ing for this interpretation would require more evidence rooted in the text itself. It should be noted, however, that this reading has the advantage of making

sense of the oft-overlooked Chapter 1, which is in fact the longest chapter of
the work. For in this chapter Anselm brings to light how the attempt to think
God reveals the human being as having the very image of God, and it points to
the very activity of thinking God (especially as something than which nothing
greater is able to be thought) both as manifesting that image and approaching
the God whom it images.[7] This reading, moreover, encourages us to step
directly into the *Proslogion*, to think dynamically and interactively alongside
Anselm so that we too will be "pleased to have come upon" the reality of God.

Anselm's manner of thinking God in the *Proslogion*
If the *Proslogion* depicts the activity of thinking God, it is natural to ask how
it does so. What kind of thinking does Anselm employ in thinking God? An
initial answer can be had by glancing at the list of chapter headings for the
Proslogion, which Anselm places just after the Preface. Twelve of the chapter
headings begin with the Latin word *quod*, "that," which suggests an assertive
mode of thinking; on the face of it, such chapters are ones in which Anselm is
making a claim or "taking a stab." Nine of them begin with the Latin word
quomodo, "in what manner," which suggests a chapter in which Anselm is
modifying, adjusting, aligning, or "endeavoring to straighten up" his thinking
in relation to God. From this we might surmise that the activity of thinking
depicted in the *Proslogion* will be an assertive, spirited straightening-up of
human thinking toward God.

    In addition, one might take into account that the *Proslogion* sprang from
a desire to unify the project of the *Monologion*, as both the Preface of the
Proslogion and Eadmer's *Life of Anselm* indicate. Recall that in the
Monologion Anselm strove to meet the demands of his brother monks, who
asked that he reach his conclusions concerning God through the "necessity of
reason." We are apt, however, to misunderstand this phrase nowadays, owing
to the cramped understanding of "reason" (and, for that matter, "necessity")
that pervades our intellectual climate. And even if we attempt to go further
back to the Schoolmen, we are still likely not to understand the phrase "necessity of reason" as Anselm did, since we might be prone to connect it directly
to Aristotelian notions of logic and "science" (*epistêmê*, *scientia*). Again, we
would be better served by looking forward from Augustine, the only person
whom Anselm names in his writings as an intellectual mentor, which he does
in the Prologue of the *Monologion*. To be sure, we can make only a brief start
here as to what "necessity of reason" means for Anselm, and yet this will be
sufficient for articulating the mode of thinking God in both the *Monologion*
and the *Proslogion*.

    In his *Soliloquies*[8] Augustine – or, more precisely, Reason itself –
describes reason (*ratio*) as *aspectus animae*,[9] "the soul's 'looking'." In *On
Order*, moreover, Augustine describes reason as *mentis motio, ea quae*

discuntur distinguendi et connectendi potens,[10] "the mind's motion, capable of distinguishing and connecting things that are learned." Reason, then, is the mind in motion, the mind actively seeking the truth by analyzing and relating things that it has already apprehended. Anselm's phrase "necessity of reason" should be taken in light of this description of reason. Reason is "on the move" when one inquires into something, such as a reality in which one believes or a reality that one wants to illuminate or explain. During such an inquiry, reason faces "moments of decision," moments when it will have to go this way or that in order to continue moving forward and digging more deeply. At such moments one should make this distinction rather than that one; or one should draw this analogy rather than some other one. The necessity at work in such a case, then, is more of a "prudential" sort than a logical one; it is a necessity grounded in reason's desire to navigate a question that makes sense in order to arrive at greater insight. (The alternative, of course, is simply to quit navigating, to cease the inquiry, to "stop thinking about it," which is what Anselm tried to do with little success with regard to concentrating the *Monologion* into a single, brief argument. This alternative is not open to those who desire to stay alive intellectually.)

It is impossible at the outset of an inquiry to specify all the factors that will determine the direction reason must take if it is going to make progress. Indeed, the path toward insight can be strewn with all sorts of unforeseen impasses (*aporiai*), and in getting past them one may have to employ sundry "tools," including logical, grammatical, pedagogical, rhetorical, ethical, and metaphysical ones. Anselm does not fret much about specifying the tools he employs in getting past the obstacles he faces; he is usually content either to identify them implicitly or to leave dialectical gaps in the reasoning process in order to draw us into his reasoning activity. This is true with regard to both the looser but more complicated chain of reasoning in the *Monologion*, and even more true with regard to the tighter, more condensed argument of the *Proslogion*. Indeed, in the latter work, the intensity of Anselm's reasoning pulls us forcefully into his *cogitatio*, his activity of thinking God, and this aspect of the work may go far toward explaining why it remains ever attractive to readers, even if ever elusive, whereas too few give adequate attention to its progenitor, the *Monologion*.

In an attempt to underscore the prudential aspect of the "necessity of reason" as Anselm sees it – i.e., that it is the sort of necessity in play when we encounter an obstacle that we *have to* overcome in the most judicious way possible if we are going to reach our destination safely – I have likely overstated the unpredictability of the activity of thinking God in the *Proslogion*. In fact, upon closer inspection, it appears that a recognizable structure of reasoning emerges in the *Proslogion*, one that can be called a "pattern of erotic thinking."[11] Such a pattern is present in Plato's *Symposium*, and it weaves it way through the Platonic tradition, which Anselm inherits primarily through Augustine. This pattern articulates the progression of a love of some reality and the yearning to obtain the whole of that reality; indeed, as Aristophanes notes in the *Symposium*, "*Eros* is the name for the spirited-desire [*epithumia*] and pursuit [*diôxis*] of the whole."[12]

Now, the wholes with which we are most familiar are the natural realities we encounter every day, which are three-dimensional in their character. If we desire to get to know such realities, we must observe them from diverse perspectives along their breadth, height, and depth.[13] Owing to such cognitive limitations, we find ourselves in a similar position when we exercise our desire to apprehend God. Yet the very unmeasuredness of God's "magnitude" or greatness demands that we apprehend him as wider, higher, and deeper than every reality within the world as well as the entire world itself – since God is, after all, something than which nothing *greater* is able to be thought. Thus the pattern of thinking God in the *Proslogion* emerges as threefold, which is unsurprising in a work by a Christian who believes in a triune God. And we can analogize this pattern not only with the trinity of breadth-height-depth, but also with the trinity of present-past-future (as Augustine might prefer) as well as the trinity of comedy-tragedy-philosophy (as Plato's Socrates in the *Symposium* suggests). It would take us too far afield here to articulate how this threefold pattern of erotic thinking makes its presence felt in the *Proslogion*; in the notes to the translation, I point to aspects of the text that evidence its presence. For now it is sufficient to suggest the comprehensive character of Anselm's approach to the God who dwells in unapproachable light. It is a comprehensiveness that in the present of thinking reaches back to the past and stretches forward to the future, thereby revealing a God who dwells under, above, and within all reality in a unique, ever-surpassing manner.

Gaunilo's objections and Anselm's reply

In addition to the *Proslogion* itself, this translation includes objections to the argument in Chapters 2–4 of the *Proslogion* written by Gaunilo ("What someone responds to these things on behalf of the fool") as well as Anselm's reply to these objections ("What the author of this little book responds to these things"). Regarding Gaunilo, we know little, only that he was a monk of the abbey of Marmoutiers and, of course, Anselm's contemporary. Anything else about Gaunilo has to be surmised from his objections to the *Proslogion*, his only extant piece of writing. It has survived because Anselm himself requested that these objections and his own reply be appended to the text of the *Proslogion* in subsequent editions. This translation honors Anselm's request.

Personally, I do not find Gaunilo's objections very compelling; for they reflect the sort of "standing-at-a-distance" or "objectifying" interpretation of the *Proslogion* that this introduction is pushing against. In other words, Gaunilo fails to involve himself in the erotic, spirited, intellectual pursuit of something than which nothing greater is able to be thought, and thus he ends up at times (such as in his "Lost Island" argument) demoting the reality of God, making the divine reality to be another "object" among "objects" – which is, to be sure, nothing more than the default mode of thinking God to which we fallen human beings daily revert. Gaunilo's failure to understand Anselm's thinking in the *Proslogion* is manifest in many ways, perhaps most obviously when he does not attend carefully to Anselm's careful wording. In his reply, Anselm calls attention to such inattentiveness as well as other defective aspects of Gaunilo's objections. More valuable than Anselm's direct response to each of Gaunilo's argument, however, is the fact that we readers are given an opportunity to share in Anselm's own reflections on what has taken place in the *Proslogion*. Indeed, perhaps it is quite fitting that Anselm's reflections on the *Proslogion* are in a sense made part of the *Proslogion* itself, inasmuch as the *Proslogion* itself both demands deep self-reflection and self-evaluation on the part of its reader (especially in Chapter 1) and capitalizes on the experience of our "self-surpassingness" as a pathway toward insight into the insurpassable self-surpassingness of God as something than which nothing greater is able to be thought. No doubt it is a stretch, but one might compare the *Proslogion*'s inclusion of Anselm's reply to the Law's inclusion of Moses' reflections on the Law in *Deuteronomy*. In both cases the "appendix" reminds the reader that there must be an ongoing return to and reflection on what is original, so that we do not forget that when it comes to divine matters, in this life we are always *in via*.

Now, we cannot know for sure exactly what Anselm saw in the exchange between Gaunilo and himself that led to his request to append it to subsequent editions of the *Proslogion*. With some surety, however, we can say that in his reply Anselm clarifies several aspects of the *Proslogion*, including his intentions as its author, the grounds for crucial distinctions he makes within it, and a way of achieving the unique thought of something than which nothing greater is able to be thought. (I call attention to a few of these clarifications in the notes.) One does not have to read these "appendices" in order to understand the *Proslogion*, because the original work is understandable on its own terms. Hence Gaunilo's objections and especially Anselm's reply are, one might say, "super-added"; they are "extra," a gift for those who want to enter more deeply into Anselm's thinking and who may need his assistance to avoid the pitfalls of the default all-too-human manner of thinking God displayed by Gaunilo. For this reason the proper response of the serious reader of the *Proslogion* is gratitude that Anselm ensured as much as he was able that his exchange with Gaunilo would be preserved for posterity.

A note on translating

Fidelity is the touchstone of translating. In this translation, therefore, I hope to have been faithful to Anselm's *Proslogion*. Fidelity in translating is not slavishness; it is, rather, steadfastness in adhering to the original thinking of the author as much as one is able. Especially when dealing with an older text, such fidelity may give rise to unconventional renderings or odd turns of phrase. But in order to allow the reader to think along with Anselm (and not simply to fit Anselm into our categories of thought), I prioritize such "literalness" over "easy readability"; for it compels the reader of Anselm's work to be alert to the complexity and depth of thought that can be encountered therein. It is undeniable, moreover, that many passages in the original *Proslogion* are very demanding on the reader, and so fidelity in translating them requires English renderings that demand serious attention on the reader's part. In a sense, this demand slaps a reader in the face in the case of the *Proslogion*, because the articulation of the central thought of the work – *aliquid quo nihil maius cogitari possit* ("something than which nothing greater is able to be thought") – forces a reader to slow down and concentrate if he does not want this phrase to become merely a term-holder in a supposed syllogism, but rather allows its signification to draw his intelligence toward alignment with the unique reality of God. Aiming primarily for readability and easy comprehension in translating the *Proslogion*, therefore, would be both an injustice to Anselm and a disservice to serious readers.

In addition, fidelity in translating a text brings out many of the human elements contained in a text. For example, compared to Anselm's writing, Gaunilo's is not as clear or crisp, and it is important that a reader experience this in English as much as possible, even if it results in apparent awkwardness. After all, there are plenty who write in English who lack clarity and crispness of expression – in short, whose English is awkward. (This introduction is the first piece of evidence of this fact!) A translation, then, should capture these features of the original text.

For the most part I have succeeded in rendering Latin words or phrases consistently with the same English word or phrase. The purpose behind this is to make clear to the English reader that certain words or phrases are repeated and thus stand out in the Latin text. I have included an appendix that lists many of the Latin words I have tried to render with consistency. In addition, with a view to prodding the English reader to think afresh along with Anselm (and not simply read the subsequent tradition back into his work), I have rendered certain words or phrases somewhat unconventionally, usually with a bow to their etymologies (e.g., *misericordia* as "pity-heartedness" rather than "mercy"). In the notes I justify some of these renderings. My hope is that readers will not be too turned off by the lack of conventionality in this regard.

It is important for understanding the *Proslogion* that the reader's thinking be adjusted to Anselm's, not vice-versa; in other words, Anselm teaches while the reader learns. My translation strives to honor this pedagogical order. More idealistically, I have striven for a translation that enables a "co-living" (*suzên*) with Anselm, if I may borrow Aristotle's notion of the proper activity of friendship. Friends "co-live," according to Aristotle, which for human beings means "co-thinking" and "co-speaking." In this translation, my attempt to be faithful to Anselm amounts to an attempt to become his friend and thereby to co-think and co-speak the *Proslogion* with him in English. To my mind, the great privilege of reading great works of past thinkers such as Anselm is that it opens up the possibility of entering into friendships with them. In the present case, Anselm's self-diffusive activity of writing the *Proslogion* has created this opening, and this translation is some small attempt to co-think with such a generous friend and to allow others to do so as well.

A note on this translation

A few aspects of this English edition of the *Proslogion* should be noted here. I have based the translation on the Latin edition of the *Proslogion* (as well as Gaunilo's objections and Anselm's reply) found in *S. Anselmi Cantuarensis Archiepiscopi Opera Omnia*, Volume I, edited by F. S. Schmitt (Stuttgart: Friedrich Frommann Verlag, 1968). In addition, I have indicated in my notes those passages in which Anselm more or less explicitly refers to a verse from the Bible, although in no way do I claim to have noted every such reference. On this score I mostly follow what Schmitt indicates in his Latin edition. In the *Proslogion*, unlike in the *Monologion*, Anselm does not feel constrained by a request of his brethren not to make use of Scripture. Yet it is not accurate to say that Anselm employs Scripture "authoritatively" in the *Proslogion*. In other words, the reader does not find "arguments from Scripture" in this work; instead, because Anselm is so steeped in the Bible – and, as a monk, he is steeped especially in the Psalms – Scriptural phrases flow freely from his pen, much as do echoes of Augustine's works. Anselm's references to Scripture, then, are natural – or, perhaps more precisely, "second-natural" – inasmuch as his own thinking is imbued with phrases, images, metaphors, and concepts garnered from the Bible. This is not to say, however, that Anselm is unaware that he is alluding to Scriptural passages when he writes, although it is to say that he intends such allusions to be persuasive not owing to their authoritative status, but simply because they shed light on what he is describing or explaining.

Hence the Scriptural dynamic in the *Proslogion* could be depicted thus: in this work (unlike in the *Monologion*), Anselm addresses God directly in the manner of prayer, and he does so in God's own "tongue," i.e., in the "language" that he and God share through Scripture. Thereby Anselm allows a

Biblical vision of both the human being and God to suffuse his activity of faith seeking understanding, not to intrude upon it. There is nothing mechanical or clunky about the *Proslogion*, a point I have tried to make already by briefly considering Anselm's understanding of the relationship between faith and reason. This same point could be made by considering Anselm's liberal and unconstrained use of Scripture in the *Proslogion*, which manifests the natural and organic character of the reasoning displayed therein. Moreover, bringing to light these aspects of the *Proslogion* indicates the "erotic" character of Anselm's thinking. The *Proslogion* is written by a man in love who wants to share with his readers precisely and comprehensively the unique vision he has of the unique God whom he loves. And in sharing this insight, Anselm reveals his thinking – indeed, his very self – in an unhindered way that bespeaks his own unity as a person and a thinker. As a whole Anselm wholeheartedly loves God as a whole, and the *Proslogion* bespeaks the underlying wholeness and harmony of Anselm himself, which makes possible his acting, as he says in the Preface, "under the person of one endeavoring to straighten up his mind toward contemplating God and seeking to understand what he believes."

In order to allow this Scriptural dynamic to come through in this translation of the *Proslogion*, I decided not to use quotation marks or italics to indicate passages from the Bible. Indeed, such indications were not present in the *Proslogion* when it was first published, and I see no reason why we who read it nowadays should be "interrupted" or "distracted" by the Scripture present in it, which quotation marks or italics have a tendency to do. Hopefully this will help the reader take the words of the *Proslogion* in their own right, as expressing the heart and mind of Anselm himself and as appealing simply to the reader's rational capacities – even if we recognize that as a matter of historical fact Anselm's own thinking was saturated with Scriptural language and notions.

In addition to notes that indicate the Scriptural passages to which Anselm refers, there are other notes that call the reader's attention to various notions, structures, allusions, and the like that are latent in the *Proslogion* or that may have been covered over in the process of translation. Taken together, these notes offer a sort of running commentary on the work, though by no means a complete one. I consider these notes to be more suggestive than assertive; they are meant to provoke the reader to consider some of the many intricacies of Anselm's thinking in the *Proslogion*. There are more notes near the beginning of the work, because it is there that Anselm introduces the basic notions and vocabulary at work in the *Proslogion* and reveals the "architecture" of his thinking, and I want to draw the reader's attention to these compelling aspects of the work. Readers are free, of course, to take or leave the comments in the notes as they deem fit.

Select bibliography

The amount of scholarship that has been dedicated to Anselm's *Proslogion* is overwhelming. Much of it focuses solely on Chapters 2–4, and much of it approaches Anselm by looking backward from Kant, Descartes, or Aquinas. I have suggested in the preceding introduction why I find such approaches problematic. What I list here, then, is just a small sample of books and articles in English (listed alphabetically by author) that aim to present the *Proslogion* (or Anselm's thought in general) in its wholeness in a manner that is not anachronistic. This list is, of course, hardly close to being comprehensive; indeed, it is embarrassingly short. This is excusable, however, since it is meant to serve only as a point of departure for any readers interested in digging more deeply into the intricacies of Anselm's thinking in the *Proslogion*. The one who is truly interested will be able to find other such sources on his own.

Colish, Marcia. *The Mirror of Language: A Study in the Medieval Theory of Knowledge*. Lincoln: University of Nebraska Press, 1983. (See especially Chapter 2: "Anselm: The Definition of the Word.")

Eadmer. *The Life of St. Anselm, Archbishop of Canterbury*. Translated by Richard Southern. Oxford: Oxford University Press, 1962.

Evans, Gillian. *Anselm and Talking About God*. Oxford: Clarendon Press, 1978.

Fournier, Michael. "Ring Structure in Chapters Six to Thirteen of Anselm's *Proslogion*." *Dionysius* 27 (2010): 127–44.

Hankey, William. "*Omnia sunt in te*: A Note on Chapters Twelve to Twenty-six of Anselm's *Proslogion*." *Dionysius* 27 (2009): 145–54.

Holopainen, Toivo. *Dialectic and Theology in the Eleventh Century*. Leiden: Brill, 1996.

Logan, Ian. *Reading Anselm's* Proslogion: *The History of Anselm's Argument and its Significance Today*. Ashgate: Farnham, 2008.

McMahon, Robert. *Understanding the Medieval Meditative Ascent: Augustine, Anselm, Boethius, and Dante*. Washington: The Catholic University of America Press, 2006.

Schufreider, Gregory. *Confessions of a Rational Mystic*. West Lafayette: Purdue University Press, 1994.

Southern, Richard. *Saint Anselm: A Portrait in a Landscape*. Cambridge: Cambridge University Press, 1990.

Sweeney, Eileen. "Anselm's *Proslogion*: The Desire for the Word." *The Saint Anselm Journal* 1 (2003): 17–31.

Sweeney, Eileen. "The Rhetoric of Prayer and Argument in Anselm." Philosophy and Rhetoric 38 (2005): 355–78.

Walz, Matthew. "An Erotic Pattern of Thinking in Anselm's *Proslogion*." *Quaestiones Disputatae* 2 (2011): 126–45.

Walz, Matthew. "The 'Logic' of Faith Seeking Understanding: A Propaedeutic for Anselm's *Proslogion*." *Dionysius* 28 (2010): 131–66.

Preface

Compelled by the prayers of some of my brothers, I previously published a small work as a model of meditating about the reason of faith in the person of someone tracking down things he does not know by reasoning silently with himself.[1] Afterwards, considering this work to be interwoven by the chaining together of many arguments, I began to seek with myself if perhaps one argument could be come upon that for proving itself would need nothing other than itself alone, and alone would suffice to build toward the following: that God truly is, and that he is the abovemost[2] good who needs no other and whom all things need so that they may be and may be well, and whatever we believe about the divine substance.[3] To this end, as I often and eagerly turned back upon thought, sometimes what I was seeking would then seem to me able to be grasped, sometimes it would flee my mind's focus[4] altogether. At last, despairing, I willed to hold back, as it were, from my searching for a reality that cannot possibly be come upon.[5] But even though I willed to close off that thought thoroughly from myself, lest by occupying my mind in vain it impede me from other things in which I would be able to make progress, it then began more and more with some forcefulness to bear itself upon me, who was willing against it and fending it off. On a certain day, therefore, while I was growing tired by vehemently resisting its forcefulness, in this very conflict of thoughts that of which I had despaired offered itself[6] in such a way that I eagerly embraced the thought that in my troubled state I had been pushing away.

Reckoning, therefore, that if it were written, what I was pleased to have come upon would be pleasing to someone reading it, I wrote the following small work about this very thing and some other things under the person of one endeavoring to straighten up his mind toward contemplating God and seeking to understand what he believes. I judged neither this book nor the one I recalled above worthy of a name or works to which an author's name should be attached, and yet because I deemed that these works should not be sent out without titles, whereby in some manner they would invite the one into whose hands they came to read them, I gave to each its own title. Thus the former was called *A Model of Meditating about the Reason of Faith*, and the latter, *Faith Seeking Understanding*.[7]

But when both works had already been copied by many with these titles, many compelled me to ascribe my name to them – especially Hugo, the reverend Archbishop of Lyons, serving as the French Apostolic Legate, who ordered me to do so by his Apostolic authority. In order that this take place more readily, I have named the former *Monologion*, that is, "soliloquy," and the latter *Proslogion*, that is, "allocution."[8]

Chapters

Proslogion

Chapter 1: Rousing[1] the mind toward contemplating God

Quick now, little man, flee a short while your occupations; hide yourself a short time from your tumultuous thoughts. Cast off your burdensome cares now, and put off until later your laborious distresses. Empty a little bit for God, and rest a little bit in him. Enter into the chamber of your mind, close off all things besides God and what may help you in seeking him, and with door closed seek him.[2] Speak now, my whole heart, speak now to God: I seek your countenance; your countenance, O Lord, I seek again.[3]

Quick now, therefore, you, Lord my God, teach my heart where and in what manner it may seek you, where and in what manner it may come upon you. Lord, if you are not here, where may I seek you, absent as you are? If, however, you are everywhere, why do I not see you, present as you are? But certainly you dwell in unapproachable light.[4] And where is unapproachable light? Or in what manner may I approach unapproachable light? Or who will lead me and lead me into it so that I may see you in it? Hence, by what signs, by what face, may I seek you?[5] Never have I seen you, Lord my God, nor have I been aware of your face. What, abovemost Lord, what will this far-away exile of yours do? What will your servant do, anxious with love of you and cast forth far from your face?[6] He pants to see you, and your face is very absent from him. He desires to approach you, and your dwelling is unapproachable. He yearns to come upon you, and he does not know your place. He longs to seek you, and he is unfamiliar with your countenance. Lord, you are my God and you are my Lord, and never have I seen you. You made me and remade me and brought all goods of mine together for me, and not yet have I been aware of you. In sum, I was made for seeing you and not yet have I made that on account of which I was made.[7]

O pitiful lot of man, since he has lost that for which he was made! O how hard and horrible that fall! Alas, what he lost and what he came upon! What withdrew and what remained! He lost the blessedness for which he was made, and he came upon a pitifulness on account of which he was not made. That withdrew without which there is nothing happy, and that remained which in itself is only pitiful. Then man was eating the bread of angels,[8] for which he hungers now; now he eats the bread of sorrows,[9] which he did not know then.

Alas, the common grief of men, the universal lament of the children of Adam! He was belching with satiety; we sigh with hunger. He was overflowing; we beg. He was happily possessing, and he pitifully deserted; we are unhappily in need, and we pitiably desire – and, alas, we remain empty! Why, when he could have done so lightly, why did he not guard for us that which we lack just as heavily? By what means did he thus block light to us and cover us in darkness? For the sake of what did he take life away from us and inflict death upon us? We afflicted ones! From where are we pushed out, where are we pushed toward? From where are we thrown down, where are we buried? From father-land into exile, from the vision of God into our blindness. From the pleasant-ness of immortality into the bitterness and horror of death. Pitiful change! From so much good into so much evil! Heavy loss, heavy sorrow, altogether heavy!

But, alas, pitiful me, one from among those pitiful children of Eve who are removed far from God! What have I begun, what have I effected? Toward what was I stretching, from what have I come? What thing am I sighing for, what things am I sighing over? I sought good things,[10] and, behold, trouble![11] I was stretching toward God, and I ran into myself. I was seeking rest in my secret place, and I came upon tribulation and sorrow in my inmost places.[12] I willed to laugh from the joy of my mind, and I am forced to bellow from the groaning of my heart.[13] Gladness was hoped for, and, behold, from this sighs are gathered together.

And O you, Lord, how long?[14] How long, Lord, do you forget us; how long do you turn your face from us?[15] When will you look back and hear us?[16] When will you enlighten our eyes and show us your face?[17] When will you restore yourself to us? Look back, Lord, hear, enlighten us, show yourself to us. Restore yourself to us, so that it may be well for us – you without whom it is just as ill for us.[18] Pity the labors and endeavors toward you undertaken by us, who avail nothing without you. You call upon us; help us.[19] I beseech you, Lord, may I not despair by sighing, but sigh forth by hoping. My heart is embittered by its desolation; I beseech you, Lord, ensweeten it by your conso-lation. Hungering, I began to seek you; I beseech you, Lord, may I not leave off, fasting. Famished, I approached you; may I not withdraw, unfed. Poor, I came toward one rich; pitiful, toward one pity-hearted;[20] may I not go back empty and scorned. And if I sigh before I eat,[21] even after these sighs, give something I may eat. Bent as I am, Lord, I am able only to look downward; straighten me up so that I may be able to stretch out upward. Gathered upon my head, my iniquities wrap around me, and as a heavy burden they make me heavy.[22] Unwrap me, unburden me, lest the well of my iniquities close its mouth over me.[23] Allow me to look upon your light, from afar or from the deep. Teach me to seek you and show yourself to the one seeking, because I am able neither to seek you unless you teach nor to come upon you unless you show yourself. May I seek you by desiring, may I desire you by seeking. May I come upon you by loving, may I love you by coming upon you.

I confess, Lord, and I give thanks, because you have created in me this your image, that remembering you, I may think you, may love you.[24] But it is so effaced by the rubbing of vices, so darkened by the smoke of sins, that it is not able to make that for which it was made unless you renew and reform it. I do not attempt, Lord, to penetrate your depth, because in no way do I compare my understanding to it; but I desire in some way to understand your truth, which my heart believes and loves. For I do not seek to understand so that I may believe, but I believe so that I may understand. For I believe this also: that unless I will have believed, I will not understand.[25]

Chapter 2: That God truly is[26]

Therefore,[27] Lord, you who give understanding to faith, give to me, as much as you know to be advantageous, so that I may understand that you *are*,[28] as we believe, and that you are what we believe. And indeed we believe that you are something than which nothing greater is able to be thought. Is it, therefore, that there is not some such nature, because the fool said in his heart: There is not a God?[29] But certainly the same fool himself, when he hears this very thing I say, "something than which nothing greater is able to be thought," understands that which he hears; and that which he understands is in his understanding, even if he may not understand that it *is*. For it is one thing for a reality to be in understanding, and another to understand a reality to be. For when a painter thinks beforehand that which is to be made, he indeed has it in understanding, but he does not yet understand that what he has not yet made *is*. When, in truth, he has already painted, he both has it in understanding and understands that what he has already made *is*. The fool too, therefore, is convinced that something than which nothing greater is able to be thought is in understanding, because he understands it when he hears it, and whatever is understood is in understanding. And certainly that than which a greater cannot be thought is not able to be in understanding alone. For if it is in understanding alone, it is able to be thought to be also in reality, which is greater. If, therefore, that than which a greater is not able to be thought is in understanding alone, then the very that than which a greater is not able to be thought is that than which a greater is able to be thought. But certainly this is not able to be. There exists, therefore, beyond doubt, something than which a greater does not avail to be thought, both in understanding and in reality.

Chapter 3: That he is not able to be thought not to be

Surely, this something than which a greater does not avail to be thought so truly *is* that it is not able to be thought not to be. For there is able to be thought something that is not able to be thought not to be, which is greater than that which is able to be thought not to be. Hence, if that than which a greater cannot be thought is able to be thought not to be, then that very that than which a greater cannot be thought is not that than which a greater cannot be thought – which is not able to fit together. Something than which a greater is not able to be thought, therefore, so truly *is* that it is not able to be thought not to be.

And this is you, Lord our God. Therefore, you so truly *are*, Lord, that you are not able to be thought not to be. And rightly so; for if some mind were able to think something better than you, a creature would ascend above the Creator and would judge about the Creator – which is very absurd. And, indeed, besides you alone, anything else that *is* is able to be thought not to be.[30] You alone, therefore, have being most truly of all and thus most greatly of all; because every other thing *is* not as truly and, accordingly, has being in a lesser way. And so why did the fool say in his heart that there is not a God, when it is so ready at hand to the rational mind that you *are* most greatly of all? Why, if not because he is dull and a fool?

Chapter 4: In what manner the fool said in his heart that which is not able to be thought

In truth, in what manner did the fool say in his heart that which he was not able to think? Or in what manner was he not able to think that which he said in his heart, since saying in the heart and thinking are the same? If this is said truly – nay, even more, if he truly both thought it because he said it in his heart and did not say it in his heart because he was not able to think it – then something is said in the heart or is thought not only in one manner. For a reality is thought otherwise when the vocal-sound signifying it is thought than when the reality itself that *is* is understood. And so in the former manner God is able to be thought not to be, whereas in the latter manner, in truth he is not able at all to be thought not to be.[31] No one, indeed, who understands that which God is, is able to think that there is not a God, although he may say these words in his heart, either without any signification or with some extraneous one. For God is that than which a greater is not able to be thought. He who understands this [i.e., that than which a greater is not able to be thought] well by all means understands this very thing so to be that not even in thought could it not be. He who understands God to be such, therefore, cannot think that he is not.

Thanks to you, good Lord, thanks to you, because that which I believed before by your granting it, I now understand by your enlightening me in such a way that even if I were to will against believing, I would not be able not to understand.

Chapter 5: That God is whatever it is better to be than not to be; and alone existing in his own right, he makes all other things from nothing

What, therefore, are you, Lord God, than which nothing greater avails to be thought? But what are you if not that abovemost of all things, alone existing in its own right, that made all other things from nothing? For whatever is not this *is* in a way that is less than is able to be thought. But this is not able to be thought about you. Which good, therefore, is apart from the abovemost good through which every good *is*? And so you are just, true, blessed, and whatever it is better to be than not to be.[32] For it is better to be just than not just, blessed than not blessed.

Chapter 6: In what manner he is capable of sensing, although he is not a body

In truth, since it is better to be capable of sensing,[33] all-able,[34] pity-hearted and incapable of suffering, than not to be, in what manner are you capable of sensing if you are not a body; or all-able if you are not able with respect to all things; or pity-hearted and simultaneously incapable of suffering? For if only bodily things are capable of sensing, because acts of sensing concern a body and are in a body, in what manner are you capable of sensing, since you are not a body but the abovemost spirit, which is better than a body?[35]

But if there is no sensing unless there is recognizing or unless it is toward recognizing – for the one who senses recognizes things in accord with what is proper to the senses, so that through sight he recognizes colors and through taste, flavors – then whatever one recognizes in some manner, one is not unfittingly said to sense in some manner. Therefore, Lord, although you are not a body, yet truly you are capable of sensing in the abovemost way – in that manner in which you recognize all things in the abovemost way, not in the manner in which an animal recognizes something by a bodily sense.[36]

Chapter 7: In what manner he is all-able, although he is not able with respect to many things

But also, in what manner are you all-able if you are not able with respect to all things? Or if you are not able to be corrupted, nor to lie, nor to make something true be false such that what was done was not done, and likewise many such things, then in what manner are you able with respect to all things?

Is it that being able with respect to such things is not ability, but inability? For one who is able with respect to such things is able with respect to that which is not advantageous to himself and with respect to that which he ought not. To the extent that one is more able with respect to such things, to the same extent adversity and perversity are more able in relation to him and he less able against adversity and perversity. One who is thus able, therefore, is able not by ability, but by inability. For he is said to be able not because he himself is able, but because his inability makes another able in relation to him. Or, "to be able" is said by a different kind of speaking, just as many things are said improperly, such as when we put "being" for "not being" and "doing" for what is a "not doing" or a "doing nothing." For we often say to one who denies that reality is a certain way, "So it is as you say it to be," when it would seem to be said more properly, "So it is not as you say it not to be." Again, we say, "He sits as he does," or, "He rests as he does," although sitting is not doing something and resting is doing nothing.[37] So also, when someone is said to have the ability of doing or suffering that which is not advantageous to himself or that which he ought not, by "ability" is understood inability, because he has this ability more inasmuch as adversity and perversity are more able in relation to him and he is more unable against them. Therefore, Lord God, you are more truly all-able, because you are able with respect to nothing through inability and nothing is able against you.

Chapter 8: In what manner he is pity-hearted and incapable of suffering

But in what manner are you simultaneously both pity-hearted and incapable of suffering?[38] For if you are incapable of suffering, you do not suffer with another; if you do not suffer with another, a pitying heart does not belong to you from suffering with someone who is pitiful – which is what being pity-hearted is. Yet, if you are not pity-hearted, from where is there so much consolation for the pitiful?

In what manner, therefore, are you and are you not pity-hearted, Lord, unless it is that you are pity-hearted with respect to us and not pity-hearted with respect to yourself? You are, indeed, pity-hearted with respect to our sensing, and you are not with respect to your own. For when you look on us pitiful ones, we sense the effect of one who is pity-hearted; you do not sense the affect. And you are pity-hearted, therefore, because you save the pitiful and spare those of yours who are sinners; and you are not pity-hearted, because you are affected by none of pity's suffering with another.

Chapter 9: In what manner he, who is just as a whole and just in the abovemost way, spares those who are evil; and that he justly pities those who are evil

In truth, in what manner do you spare those who are evil, if you are just as a whole and just in the abovemost way?[39] For in what manner does one who is just as a whole and in the abovemost way do something not just? Or what justice is it to give everlasting life to one who merits eternal death? From where, therefore, good God – good to those who are good and to those who are evil – from where does it belong to you to save those who are evil, if this is not just and you do not do anything not just?

Is it that this hides in the unapproachable light in which you dwell because your goodness is incomprehensible?[40] Truly in the deepest and most secret place of your goodness hides a spring from which flows the river of your pity-heartedness. For although you are just as a whole and in the abovemost way, yet on that account you are also well-disposed to those who are evil, because you are good as a whole in the abovemost way. For you would be less good if you were well-disposed to none who are evil. For one who is good both to those who are good and to those who are evil is better than one who is good only to those who are good. And one who is good to those who are evil both by punishing and by sparing is better than one who is good to those who are evil only by punishing. For this reason, therefore, you are pity-hearted: because you are good as a whole and in the abovemost way. And although it perhaps seems evident why you would give back good things to those who are good and evil things to those who are evil, certainly this is thoroughly to be wondered at: why you, who are just as a whole and in need of nothing, would give good things to those of yours who are evil and guilty. O depth of your goodness, God! That from which you are pity-hearted is seen, and yet it is not seen all through. And that from which the stream flows is discerned, and yet the spring from which it is born is not perceived all through. For from the fullness of goodness you are kind to those of yours who are sinners, and yet in the depth of goodness hides the reason why this is so.[41] For although it is out of goodness that you give back good things to those who are good and evil things to those who are evil, yet the reason of justice seems to demand this. Yet, in truth, when you give good things to those who are evil, it is known that one who is good in the abovemost way has willed to do this, and yet it is a wonder why one who is just in the abovemost way was able to will this.

O pity-heartedness, from what wealthy sweetness and sweet wealth you flow forth to us! O unmeasuredness of God's goodness, by what affect you should be loved by sinners! For you save the just when justice accompanies them, while you set sinners free when justice condemns them – the former by means of merits that help them, the latter by means of merits that counteract them; the former while they recognize the goods you gave, the latter even while they do not recognize the evils you hated. O unmeasured goodness, which thus exceeds every understanding, may that pity-heartedness which proceeds from so much wealth of yours come over me! May that which flows forth from you flow into me! Spare through your clemency, lest you avenge through your justice! For even if it is difficult to understand in what manner your pity-heartedness is not apart from your justice, it is nonetheless necessary to believe that what pours forth out of goodness is never turned against justice. Indeed, this goodness is nothing without justice – nay, even more, it accords truly with justice. For if you are pity-hearted because you are just in the abovemost way, and you are not good in the abovemost way unless because you are just in the abovemost way, then truly on this account you are pity-hearted because you are just in the abovemost way.[42] Help me, just and pity-hearted God, whose light I seek; help me, so that I may understand what I say. Truly, therefore, it is for this reason that you are pity-hearted: because you are just.

Is not your pity-heartedness, therefore, born out of your justice? Do you not spare those who are evil, therefore, out of justice? If it is thus, Lord, if it is thus, teach me in what manner it is. Is it that it is just that you are so good that you cannot be understood as better, and that it is just that you work so ably that you are not able to be thought more able? For what is more just than this? Indeed, this would not come to be if you were good only by paying back and not by sparing, and if you made good men only out of those who are not good and not also out of those who are evil. And so in this manner it is just that you spare those who are evil and that you make good men out of those who are evil. In sum, that which does not come to be justly ought not come to be, and that which ought not come to be comes to be unjustly. If, therefore, you pity those who are evil not justly, you ought not pity; and if you ought not pity, you pity unjustly. And if saying this is impermissible, yet it is permissible to believe that you justly pity those who are evil.

Chapter 10: In what manner he justly punishes and justly spares those who are evil

But it is also just that you punish those who are evil. For what is more just than that those who are good receive good things and those who are evil receive evil things? In what manner, therefore, is it both just that you punish those who are evil and just that you spare those who are evil?

Is it that in one manner you justly punish those who are evil and in another manner you justly spare those who are evil? For when you punish those who are evil, it is just because it fits with their merits; whereas when you spare those who are evil, it is just because it is becoming not to their merits, but to your goodness. For by sparing those who are evil, you are thus just with respect to yourself and not with respect to us, just as you are pity-hearted with respect to us and not with respect to yourself. Hence, by saving us whom you might justly destroy: just as you are pity-hearted not because you feel an affect, but because we feel an effect, so also you are just not because you render to us what is owed, but because you do what is becoming to yourself as good in the abovemost way. So in this way without contrariety you justly punish and you justly spare.

Chapter 11: In what manner all the ways of the Lord are pity-heartedness and truth,[43] and yet the Lord is just in all his ways[44]

But can it also be that it is not just with respect to yourself, Lord, that you punish those who are evil? Indeed, it is just that you are so just that you cannot be thought more just. This would never be so if you were only to render good things to those who are good and not to render evil things to those who are evil. For one who pays back things merited both to those who are good and to those who are evil is more just than one who pays back things merited

only to those who are good. Therefore, it is just with respect to yourself, just
and well-disposed God, both when you punish and when you spare. Truly,
therefore, all the ways of the Lord are pity-heartedness and truth,[45] and yet
the Lord is just in all his ways.[46] And certainly this is without contrariety,
because it is not just that those whom you will to punish be saved, and it is
not just that those whom you will to spare be condemned. For that alone is
just which you will, and that is not just which you do not will.[47] So, therefore,
your pity-heartedness is born from your justice, because it is just that you are
good in such a way that you are good also by sparing. And this is, perhaps,
why one who is just in the abovemost way is able to will good things for those
who are evil. But if to any extent it is able to be grasped why you are able to
will to save those who are evil, it certainly is able to be comprehended by no
reason why you save these rather than those from like evils through the abovemost goodness and why you condemn those rather than these through the
abovemost justice.

So, therefore, you are capable of sensing, all-able, pity-hearted, and incapable of suffering, just as you are living, wise, good, blessed, eternal, and whatever it is better to be than not to be.[48]

Chapter 12: That God is the life itself by which he lives, and so also about like things

But certainly it is not through something other than yourself that you are whatever you are. You are, therefore, the life itself by which you live, and the wisdom by which you wisely know, and the goodness by which you are good to
those who are good and to those who are evil; and so also regarding like things.

Chapter 13: In what manner he alone is uncircumscribed and eternal, although other spirits are uncircumscribed and eternal

But each thing that is enclosed in some manner in place and in time is less than
that which no law of place or of time constrains. Since, therefore, nothing is
greater than you, no place or time contains you, but you are everywhere and
always. Because this can be said regarding you alone, you alone are

uncircumscribed and eternal. In what manner, therefore, are other spirits also said to be uncircumscribed and eternal?

And, indeed, you alone are eternal, because you alone of all, just as you do not cease to be, so you do not begin to be. But in what manner are you alone uncircumscribed? Is it that compared to you a created spirit is circumscribed, whereas compared to a body it is uncircumscribed? For what is altogether circumscribed is that which, when it is somewhere as a whole, is not able to be elsewhere simultaneously; this is discerned regarding only things that are bodily. Indeed, what is uncircumscribed is that which is everywhere as a whole simultaneously; this is understood regarding you alone. But what is simultaneously circumscribed and uncircumscribed is that which, when it is somewhere as a whole, is able simultaneously to be elsewhere as a whole, although it is not able to be everywhere; this is recognized regarding created spirits. For if the soul as a whole were not in the singular members of its body, it would not as a whole sense in those singular members. You, therefore, Lord, are singularly uncircumscribed and eternal, and yet other spirits as well are uncircumscribed and eternal.

Chapter 14: In what manner and why God is seen and is not seen by those seeking him

Is it, my soul, that you have come upon that which you were seeking? You were seeking God, and you have come upon this: something that of all things is the abovemost, than which nothing better is able to be thought; and this something is life, light, wisdom, goodness, eternal blessedness itself; and this something is everywhere and always. For if you have not come upon your God, in what manner is he that which you have come upon and that which you have understood with so certain a truth and so true a certainty? If, indeed, you have come upon him, why is it that you do not sense that which you have come upon? Why, Lord God, does my soul not sense you if it has come upon you?

Is it that my soul has not come upon that which it has come upon as being light and truth? For in what manner did my soul understand that which it has come upon except by seeing light and truth? Or would it be able to understand anything about you at all except through your light and your truth?[49] If, therefore, my soul has seen light and truth, it has seen you. If it has not seen you, it has not seen light or truth. Is it that both light and truth are that which my soul has seen, and nonetheless it has not yet seen you, because it has seen you to some extent, but it has not seen you as you are?[50]

Lord my God, you who have formed me and reformed me, say to my

desiring soul what you are other than that which it has seen, so that it may
see purely that which it desires. It stretches itself out so that it may see more,
and it sees nothing but darkness beyond that which it has seen. Nay, even
more, it does not see darkness, of which there is none in you,[51] but it sees
itself as not able to see any more on account of its own darkness. Why is this,
Lord, why is this? Is its eye darkened by its own sickness, or is it beat back
by your brightness? But certainly it is both darkened in itself and beat back
by you. Indeed, it is both obscured by its minuteness and overwhelmed by
your unmeasuredness. Truly, it is both constricted by its narrowness and conquered by your ampleness. For how much that light is, from which glimmers
every true thing that enlightens the rational mind! How ample that truth is,
in which there is all that is true and outside of which there is only nothing
and what is false! How unmeasured is that which sees with one gaze whatever things have come to be, and by which and through which and in what
manner they came to be from nothing! What purity, what simplicity, what
certainty and splendor are there! Certainly more than avails to be understood
by a creature.

Chapter 15: That he is greater than is able to be thought

Therefore, Lord, not only are you that than which a greater cannot be
thought, but you are something greater than is able to be thought.[52] For since
being something of this sort avails to be thought, if you are not this very
thing, something greater than you is able to be thought, which cannot come
about.

Chapter 16: That this is the unapproachable light[53] in which you dwell

Truly, Lord, this is the unapproachable light in which you dwell. For truly there
is not something else that might penetrate this in such a way that there it may
see you all through. Truly, for this reason I do not see this light: because it is
too much for me; and yet whatever I do see, I see through it, just as a sick eye
that sees sees through the sun's light, which it cannot look at in the sun itself.
My understanding is not able with respect to this light. It shines too brightly;
the eye of my soul does not grasp it, nor does it endure stretching out toward
it for long. It is beat back by its brightness, it is conquered by its ampleness, it

is overwhelmed by its unmeasuredness, it is confounded by its capaciousness. O abovemost and unapproachable light, O whole and blessed truth, how far you are from me, who am so close to you! How remote you are from my view, the view of one who is so present to your view! You are present everywhere as a whole, and I do not see you. In you I move and in you I am,[54] and I am not able to approach you. You are within me and around me, and I do not sense you.

Chapter 17: That in God there is harmony, odor, flavor, softness, and beauty, each in its own inexpressible manner

Still, Lord, in your light and blessedness, you are hiding from my soul, and on that account it is still moving about in its darkness and pitifulness. For it looks around, and it does not see your beauty. It listens, and it does not hear your harmony. It smells, and it does not perceive your odor. It tastes, and it does not recognize your flavor. It feels, and it does not sense your softness. For you have these things in yourself, Lord God, in your own inexpressible manner – you who have given them to created realities in their own sensible manner.[55] But the senses of my soul have stiffened, they have become dull, they have been blocked up by the ancient weariness of sin.

Chapter 18: That there are no parts in God or in his eternity, which is himself

And again, behold, trouble; again, behold, mourning and grief block the way of one who is seeking joy and gladness! My soul was hoping now for satedness and, behold, it is overwhelmed again by neediness! It was longing now to eat and, behold, it is starting to hunger more! I was endeavoring to rise up toward God's light, and I fell back into my darkness. Nay, even more, I did not fall into it just now, but I sense myself wrapped up in it. I fell before my mother conceived me. Certainly I was conceived in it,[56] and I was born with it enwrapping me. Certainly we all once fell in him in whom we all sinned.[57] In him – who was easily possessing and who wickedly lost for himself and for us – in him we all lost that which we do not know when we will to seek it, that which we do not come upon when we seek, that which is not what we are seeking when we come upon it. Help me, Lord, on account of your goodness.[58] I have sought your countenance; your countenance, Lord, I will seek again. Turn not your face from me.[59] Lift me up from myself toward you. Cleanse, heal, focus, enlighten the eye of my mind,[60] so that it may gaze on you. May my soul gather its powers together again and may it stretch out again with its whole understanding toward you, Lord.

What are you, Lord, what are you? What will my heart understand you to be? Certainly you are life, you are wisdom, you are truth, you are goodness, you are blessedness, you are eternity, and you are every true good. These are many things; my narrow understanding cannot see simultaneously with a gaze so one that it delights in all of them simultaneously. In what manner, therefore, Lord, are you all these? Is it that they are parts of you, or rather that each one of them is that which you are as a whole? For whatever is joined with parts is not altogether one, but in some manner is many and diverse by itself, and can be loosened up either actually or in understanding – which things are foreign to you than whom nothing better is able to be thought. There are, therefore, no parts in you, Lord, nor are you many; rather, you are something so one and the same with your very self that in no way are you unlike to your very self. Nay, even more, you are oneness itself, divisible by no understanding. Life and wisdom and the rest, therefore, are not parts of you, but are all one, and each one of them is that which you are as a whole and that which all the rest are. Because, therefore, you do not have parts, and neither does your eternity that you are, there is nowhere and never a part of you or of your eternity; rather, you are everywhere as a whole, and your whole eternity is always.

Chapter 19: That he is not in place or time, but all things are in him

But if through your eternity you were and are and will be, and to-have-been is not to-be-going-to-be, and to-be is neither to-have-been nor to-be-going-to-be, then in what manner is your whole eternity always?

Is it that nothing passes from your eternity such that it now is not, nor is there something going to be as if it were not yet? There has not been a yesterday, therefore, and there will not be a tomorrow, but you are yesterday and today and tomorrow. Nay, even more, you are neither yesterday nor today nor tomorrow, but you are simply outside all time. For yesterday and today and tomorrow are nothing other than in time; however, although there is nothing without you, you are not in place or time, but all are in you. For nothing contains you, but you contain all.

Chapter 20: That he is before and beyond all things, even eternal things

You, therefore, fill and embrace all things; you are before and beyond all things.[61] And, indeed, you are before all things, because before they came to be, you are. Truly, in what manner are you beyond all things? For how are you beyond those things that will not have an end?

Is it that those things can in no way be without you, whereas you are in no manner less even if they go back into nothing? For in this way you are beyond them in some manner. Is it also that those things can be thought to have an end while you never can? For thus indeed these things have an end in some manner, whereas in no manner do you have an end. And certainly that which in no manner has an end is beyond that which in some manner is determined by an end. Is it, moreover, that in this manner you pass beyond all things, even eternal things, in that eternity as a whole, yours and theirs, is present to you, although they do not yet have from their own eternity that which is going to come about, just as they no longer have that which is past? So, indeed, you are always beyond them, since you are always present there, or since that at which they have not yet arrived is always present to you.

Chapter 21: Whether this is an age of an age or ages of ages

Is this, therefore, an age of an age or ages of ages? For just as an age of times contains all temporal things, so your eternity contains even the very ages of times. Indeed, this eternity is an age, on account of its indivisible oneness, while it is also ages, on account of its unboundable unmeasuredness. And although you are so great, Lord, that all are full of you and are in you, yet you are without all space, so that in you there is neither a middle nor a half nor any part at all.

Chapter 22: That he alone is what he is and who he is

You alone, therefore, Lord, are what you are, and you are who you are. For that which is one thing in the whole and another in its parts, as well as that in which there is something changeable, is not altogether what it is. And that which began from not-being and is able to be thought not to be; and that which, unless it subsists through another, goes back into not-being; and that which has a having-been that it no longer is as well as a going-to-be that it not yet is: properly and absolutely, it is not. You, indeed, are what you are, because whatever you are at some time or in some manner, this you are as a whole and always.

And you are who you are properly and simply, because you have neither a having-been nor a going-to-be, but only present being; nor are you able to be thought not to be at some time. And you are life and light and wisdom and blessedness and eternity and many good things of this sort, and yet you aren't anything but the one and abovemost good, altogether sufficient for yourself, needing nothing, that which all things need so that they may be and so that they may be well.

Chapter 23: That this good is equally Father and Son and Holy Spirit; and this is the one thing necessary, which is every and the whole and the only good

You are this good, God the Father; your Word, that is, your Son, is this good. For in the Word by which you speak your very self, there is not able to be something other than that which you are, or something greater or less than you, because your Word is true in that very manner in which you are truth-ful; and on this account your Word is, as you are, truth itself, not a truth other than you; and thus you are simple, such that from you there is not able to be born something other than that which you are. This very thing is love, one and common to you and your Son; it is the Holy Spirit proceeding from both of you. For the same love is not unequal to you or to your Son, because as much as you are and he is, so much do you love yourself and him, and so much does he love you and himself. There is not anything else from you and from him that is not unequal to you and to him; nor is there able to proceed from the abovemost simplicity anything else that is the same as that from which it proceeds. Now, what each single someone is, this the whole Trinity is simultaneously, Father and Son and Holy Spirit; because each single some-one is not other than oneness that is simple in the abovemost way and sim-plicity that is one in the abovemost way, which is not able to be multiplied nor able to be one thing and another.

Furthermore, this is the one thing necessary.[62] Furthermore, this is that one thing necessary in which there is every good. Nay, even more, it is every and the one and the whole and the only good.

Chapter 24: Conjecturing[63] of what sort and how much this good is

Rouse up, now, my soul, and straighten up your whole understanding, and, as much as you are able, think of what sort and how much that good is. For if single goods are delightful, think intensely how delightful that good is which contains the pleasantness of all goods.[64] And we have not experienced pleasantness of this sort in created realities; rather, it is a pleasantness that differs as much as the Creator differs from the creature. For if created life is good, how good is creative life? If salvation that has been made is pleasant, how pleasant is the salvation that makes every salvation? If wisdom in the recognition of created realities is lovable, how lovable is the wisdom that establishes all things from nothing? In sum, if there are many and great delights in delightful realities, of what sort and how much is the delight in him who made those delightful things themselves?

Chapter 25: What and how many are the goods for those who enjoy this?[65]

O the one who enjoys this good! What it will be to him, and what it will not be! Certainly whatever he wills will be, and that which he wills against will not be. Indeed, goods of the body and the soul will be there, of the sort that neither eye has seen nor ear heard nor the heart of man has thought.[66] Why, therefore, do you wander through many things, little man, by seeking the goods of your soul and your body?[67] Love one good, in which all goods are, and it suffices. Desire the simple good, which is every good, and it is enough. For what do you love, what do you desire, my soul? It is there; whatever you love, whatever you desire, is there.

If beauty delights: the just will be bright as the sun.[68] If speed or strength, or the freedom of a body that nothing can obstruct: they will be like the angels of God,[69] because an animal body is sown, and a spiritual body will rise,[70] by a power, indeed, that is not from nature. If long and healthy life: healthful eternity and eternal health are there, because the just will live forever and the salvation of the just comes from the Lord.[71] If satedness: they will be sated when the glory of God appears.[72] If inebriatedness: they will be inebriated from the abundance of the house of God.[73] If melody: there the choirs of angels sing to God without end. If any pleasure whatsoever that is not unclean but clean: God will give them drink from the torrent of his pleasure.[74]

If wisdom: God's very wisdom will show itself to them. If friendship: they will love God more than themselves and one another as themselves, and God will love them more than they love themselves, because they love him and themselves and one another through him, and he loves himself and them through himself. If concord: there will be one will for all, because there will be no will for them except the will of God. If ability: they will be all-able of their own will as God is of his. For just as God will be able to do what he wills through himself, so they will be able to do what they will through him, because just as they shall will nothing other than what he shall will, so he shall will whatever they shall will, and what he shall will, will not be able not to be. If honor and riches: God will set his own good and faithful servants over many things.[75] Nay, even more, they will be and will be called sons of God and gods,[76] and where his Son will be, there also they will be, heirs indeed of God, but Christ's coheirs.[77] If true security: certainly they will be certain that never or in no way will this – or rather this good – fail them in the future, just as they will be certain that they themselves will not voluntarily lose it, nor that the loving God will remove it from those beloved whom he called, nor that something more able than God will separate God and those who have been called.

Indeed, of what sort and how much is that joy where there is such and so much good? Human heart, needy heart, heart that has experienced hardships – nay, even more, heart that has been buried by hardship: how much will you rejoice if you abound with all these things? Ask your inmost being if it can grasp the joy it has from so much blessedness belonging to it. But certainly if anyone else whom you love altogether as yourself were to have the same blessedness, your joy would be doubled, because you would rejoice no less for him than for yourself. If, indeed, two or three or many more were to have this very thing, you would rejoice just as much for each as you do for yourself, if you love each as you love yourself. Therefore, in that complete charity of the innumerable blessed angels and men, where no one loves another less than oneself, everyone will rejoice no differently for each other than for oneself. If, therefore, the heart of man will barely grasp the joy it has from its own good alone, in what manner will it be capable of so many and such great joys? And, indeed, because everyone rejoices regarding the good of another to the extent that he loves the other: just as in that complete happiness everyone will love God incomparably more than himself and all others with him, so he will rejoice regarding God's happiness inestimably more than regarding his own or that of all others with him. But if they love God with their whole heart, whole mind, whole soul, yet such that the whole heart, whole mind, whole soul does not suffice for the dignity of that love,[78] then surely they will rejoice with their whole heart, whole mind, whole soul, such that the whole heart, whole mind, whole soul does not suffice for the fullness of grace.

Chapter 26: Is this the full joy that the Lord promises?

My God and my Lord, my hope and the joy of my heart, say to my soul whether this is the joy about which you spoke to us through your Son: Ask and you will receive, that your joy may be full.[79] For I have come upon a certain full joy, and one more than full. Indeed, with heart full, mind full, soul full, the whole man full of that joy, joy will still exceed above measure. It is not, therefore, that that whole joy will enter into those rejoicing, but that all those rejoicing will enter into joy. Say, Lord, say to your servant interiorly in his heart whether this is the joy in which your servants will enter, who enter into the joy of their Lord.[80] But certainly with regard to that joy whereby your chosen ones will rejoice, neither eye has seen nor ear heard nor has it arisen in the heart of man.[81] Not yet, therefore, Lord, have I said or thought how much those blessed of yours will rejoice. Indeed, as much as they will love, so much will they rejoice; as much as they will recognize, so much will they love. How much will they recognize you then, Lord, and how much will they love? Certainly in this life neither eye has seen nor ear heard nor has it arisen in the heart of man how much they will recognize you and love you in that life.[82]

I pray, God, that I may recognize you, may love you, so that I may rejoice regarding you. And if I am not able to do so in this life to the full, may I indeed make progress until those days when it may come to the full. May awareness of you make progress in me here, and there may it become full; may your love grow in me here, and there may it be full, so that my great joy may be in hope here, and there it may be full in reality. Lord, through your Son you help us – nay, even more, you counsel us – to ask, and you promise we will receive, so that our joy may be full.[83] I ask, Lord, for that which you counsel through our admirable Counselor; may I receive that which you promise through your truth, so that my joy may be full.[84] Meanwhile, may my mind meditate thereon, may my tongue speak therefrom. May my heart love it, may my mouth talk about it. May my soul thirst for it, may my flesh hunger for it, may my whole substance desire it, until I may enter into the joy of my Lord,[85] who is the triune and one God blessed unto ages. Amen.[86]

Gaunilo's Objections

"What someone responds to these things on behalf of the fool"

[1] To the one who doubts whether there is or denies that there is some such nature than which nothing greater is able to be thought, it is said that this nature is proved to be as follows: First of all, the very one who denies or questions regarding it has it in understanding, since the one who hears it when it is said understands what has been said. Next, it is necessary that what he understands is not in the understanding alone, but is in reality as well. This is proved as follows: It is greater to be in reality as well than in understanding alone, and if it is in understanding alone, anything that is in reality as well will be greater than it. And so that which is greater than all things will be less than something and will not be greater than all things – which is certainly contradictory. For this reason it is necessary that that which is greater than all things, which has already been proved to be in understanding, is not in understanding alone, but in reality as well, because otherwise it will not be able to be greater than all things.

[2] Perhaps one is able to respond thus:

"This is said to be already in my understanding on account of nothing else except that I understand that which is said. Could I not likewise be said to have in understanding any false things whatsoever as well as things that exist in their own right in no manner at all, since when someone says them I would understand whatever things he would say? Unless perhaps it is established that this thing is able to be had in thought not in that manner in which any false or dubious thing is able to be had; and then for this reason I am not said to think it or to have it in thought when it is heard, but instead I am said to understand it or to have it in understanding, because I would not be able to think this thing in any other way except by understanding that it exists, that is, by comprehending with knowledge that it exists in reality itself.

"But if this is the case, then, first of all, it will not be one thing already to have this same thing in understanding at an earlier time and another to understand that it is at a later time, as happens in the case of a picture that is first in the soul of the painter and then later in the work. Moreover, it will scarcely be able to be believed that when it has been said and heard, it is not able to be thought not to be in the very manner in which God too is not able to be thought not to be. For if it is not able to be thought not to be, why is this whole dispute taken up against one who denies or doubts that there is some such nature? Lastly, it should be proved to me by some indubitable argument that as soon as it is thought, it is not able to be perceived except with certainty regarding its indubitable existence. This should be proved to me not by the fact that it is already in my understanding when I understand what is heard, because I still think that in like manner there may be able to be any number of other uncertain or even false things said by someone whose words I understand. This is the case even more so if, as often happens, I were to believe these words while I was being deceived – I, who do not yet believe regarding the present case.

[3] "Hence, that example about the painter who already has in understanding a picture that he is about to make is not able to fit with this argument sufficiently. For that picture, before it came to be, is possessed in the very artistic skill of the painter, and any such thing in the artistic skill of an artisan is nothing other than a part of his intelligence; because even as St. Augustine says, 'When a carpenter is about to make a chest as a product, he has it beforehand in his artistic skill. The chest that comes about as a product is not alive, whereas the chest that is in the artistic skill is alive; for the artisan's soul lives, and in his soul are all these things before they are brought forth.'[1] For how are they alive in the living soul of the artisan unless because they are nothing other than that very soul's knowledge or intelligence? Yet, in truth, beyond those things that are known to pertain to the nature itself of the mind, anything else is perceived by the understanding to be true either when it is heard or when it is thought about. And without doubt, that which is true is one thing, while the understanding by which it is grasped is another. On account of this, even if it is true that there is something than which anything greater cannot be thought, when it is heard and understood, it is nonetheless not of the same sort as a picture in a painter's understanding that has not yet been made.

[4] "At this point one may add the following, which was already suggested above: Regarding this thing that is greater than all that are able to be thought – which is said to be able to be nothing other than God himself – no more am I able to think it or to have it in understanding in relation to a reality I am aware of from its species or its genus, than I am able to think or to have in understanding God himself – whom, at any rate, on account of this very fact, I am able by all means to think not to be. For neither have I been aware of this very thing, nor am I able to conjecture it from another thing like it, since even you assert it to be such that there cannot be anything like it. For if I were to hear something said about a man of whom I am utterly unaware, of whom I was not even aware that he *is*, I could think about him according to the reality itself that man is, that is, through that specific or general awareness by which

I am aware of what man is or what men are. And yet, if the one who had spoken were lying, it could come about that the man about whom I was thinking does not exist, although I nonetheless thought of him in relation to a true reality, which would not be the man himself, but is any man whatsoever.

"So, therefore, when I hear 'God' or 'something greater than all things' said, I cannot have it in thought or in understanding in the way that I would have something false in thought or in understanding. Even though I am able to think this false thing in relation to a reality that is true and of which I am aware, I cannot have 'God' or 'something greater than all things' except in relation to its vocal sound alone, and according to that alone, something is hardly or never able to be thought of as true. If indeed it is thought of in relation to its vocal sound alone, it is not so much that one thinks of the vocal sound itself – which is a reality and by all means true (i.e., the sound of the letters and of the syllables) – as that one thinks of the signification of the vocal sound that is heard. Yet this would be thought not as if by someone who is aware of what is usually signified by that vocal sound, namely, by someone by whom it is thought of in relation to a reality or as something true in thought alone. In truth, it would be thought as if by someone who is not aware of it and only thinks of it in relation to the motion of the soul that is brought about by the hearing of that vocal sound and that provokes him to fashion for himself a signification of that perceived vocal sound. What a wonder it would be if one were ever capable of the truth of reality in this way! So, therefore, when I hear and understand someone who says that there is something greater than all the things that avail to be thought, it does not establish right away that this is held in any other way except in my understanding. So much, then, regarding the claim that the abovemost nature is said to be in my understanding.

[5] "But that such a nature is also in reality is then proved to me because if it were not in reality, whatever is in reality will be greater than it, and thereby it will not be that which is greater than all things – which, at any rate, was already proved to be in understanding. To this I respond: If it should be said that there is something that cannot even be thought in relation to the truth of any reality, I do not deny that in this way it is in my understanding. But because one is not able in any way to reach the fact that there is such a thing in reality as well, I do not thoroughly concede to him that there is such a thing until it is proven to me by an indubitable argument.

"When he says that that which is greater than all things *is*, or otherwise it will not be greater than all things, he does not attend enough to whom he is speaking. For I do not yet say – rather, I even deny or doubt – that something greater than any true reality *is*; nor do I concede any being to it other than when (if this should be called 'being') the soul endeavors to fashion a reality of which it is utterly unaware only in relation to a vocal sound that it has heard. In what manner, therefore, is it proved to me that this greater thing subsists in the truth of reality from the fact that it is established that it is greater than all things? For I may even deny or at least doubt that this has been established, so that neither in my understanding nor in my thought will I say that this greater thing *is*, not even in that manner in which many doubtful and uncertain things *are*. For first it is necessary that it become certain to me that this greater thing is somewhere in true reality, and then at last, from the fact that it is greater than all things, it will not be questionable that it also subsists in itself.

[6] "For example, some people say that somewhere in the ocean there is an island that some name the 'Lost Island,' owing to the difficulty – or, rather, the impossibility – of coming upon that which is not. This island is fabled to prosper with an inestimable abundance of all riches and delights, even more than the Isles of the Blessed; and having no owner or inhabitant, it is fabled to stand out among all other lands in which men dwell with its overflow of things to be possessed. So someone might say to me that there is this island, and I might easily understand what is said as having no difficulty in it. And then if he were to add as a consequence and say, 'You are not able to doubt further that such an island – which is more outstanding than all other lands and which you do not question to be in your understanding – truly is in reality somewhere. And because it is more outstanding, it is not in understanding alone, but is also in reality. For this reason, then, it is necessary that it *is*; because unless it were to be, any other land that is in reality will be more outstanding than it, and so that very thing already understood by you as more outstanding will not be more outstanding.' – I say that if by these means he wanted me to build toward the fact that concerning this island it is not to be questioned further that it truly *is*, either I would believe that he is joking or I know not whom I ought to believe more foolish: myself, if I were to concede this to him; or him, if he deemed that he had built toward the being of this island with some certainty, unless he had first taught that its outstandingness is in my understanding only in the manner in which a reality existing truly and undoubtedly is, and not in any manner in which something false or uncertain is."

[7] With these words, then, that fool might respond to the objections raised against him. And when it is asserted next that this greater thing is such that it does not avail to be in thought alone, and further that this is proved in no other way than that otherwise it will not be greater than all things, that same fool would be able to refer to this very response and say: "For when did I say that there is such a something – that is, a greater than all things – in the truth of reality, such that therefrom it ought to be clear to me as proven that it is also in reality itself, so much so that it is not able to be thought not to be? On this account, it should first be proved by a most certain argument that there is some nature that is more above – that is, a nature greater and better than all things that are – so that therefrom we would now be able to prove as well that it does not lack all those things that something greater or better than all things must be."

When, however, it is said that this abovemost reality cannot be *thought* not to be, perhaps it would be better said that it is not able to be *understood* not to be, or even that it is not able to be *understood* to be able not to be. For according to the proper sense of the word, false things cannot be *understood*, though they are able at any rate to be *thought* in that manner in which the fool thought that there is not a God. And besides, I know most certainly that I am, but I nonetheless know also that I am able not to be. Indeed, I understand undoubtingly that what is abovemost – namely, God – both *is* and is not able not to be. I do not know, however, if I am able to think that I am not, as long as I know most certainly that I am. But if I am able, why am I not able also to think that anything else that I know with that same certainty is not? If, however, I am not able, then this will no longer be something proper to God.

[8] The remaining parts of this little book are magnificently explained so truthfully and so clearly, and in fact are replete with usefulness and a fragrance with that inmost odor of a pious and holy affect, that in no manner are these remaining parts to be scorned on account of those things in the opening parts that are indeed sensed rightly but argued less firmly; rather, those things in the opening parts should be argued more robustly, and thus all the parts should be received with unabated veneration and praise.

Anselm's Reply

"What the author of this little book responds to these things"

Since the fool, against whom I spoke in my little work, is not the one who reprehends me in these things that were said, but rather someone who is not foolish and who is a Catholic Christian speaking on behalf of the fool, it is able to suffice for me to respond to a Catholic Christian.

[I] Indeed, you say – whoever you are who say these things – that the fool is able to say that something than which a greater is not able to be thought is not in understanding in any way other than something that cannot even be thought in relation to the truth of any reality is in understanding. Also, the fool is able to say this: it no more follows that what I call "that than which a greater is not able to be thought" is in reality from the fact that it is in understanding, than it follows that the Lost Island most certainly exists from the fact that the one hearing it described in words does not question that it is in his understanding.

In truth, I say this: If that than which a greater is not able to be thought neither is understood or thought, nor is in understanding or in thought, then surely: either God is not that than which a greater is not able to be thought; or he neither is understood or thought, nor is in understanding or in thought. I use your faith and your conscience as the strongest argument that this is quite false. That than which a greater is not able to be thought, therefore, truly is understood and thought, and is in understanding and in thought. Hence, either the claims by which you are endeavoring to prove the contrary are not true, or what you opine to conclude from them as a consequence does not follow.[1]

Now, you deem that from the fact that something than which a greater cannot be thought is understood, it does not follow that it is in understanding; and you hold that it does not follow that it is in reality from the fact that it is in understanding. To this, I certainly say that if it is even able to be thought to be, it is necessary that it *is*. For that than which a greater cannot be thought is not able to be thought to be except as without a starting-point. But whatever is able to be thought to be and is not, is able to be thought to be through a starting-point. It is not the case, therefore, that that than which a greater cannot be thought is able to be thought to be and is not. If, therefore, it is able to be thought to be, of necessity it *is*.

Furthermore, if, at any rate, it is able even to be thought, it is necessary that it *is*. For no one who denies or doubts that something than which a greater is not able to be *is*, denies or doubts that if there were such a thing, neither in actuality nor in understanding would it be able not to be. For otherwise it would not be that than which a greater is not able to be thought. But regarding whatever is able to be thought and is not: if it *is*, it is able not to be either in actuality or in understanding. Hence, if it is able even to be thought, that than which a greater cannot be thought is not able not to be. But let us propose that it is not, even if it avails to be thought. Yet regarding whatever is able to be thought and is not: if it *is*, it would not be that than which a greater is not able to be thought. If, therefore, it were that than which a greater is not able to be thought, it would not be that than which a greater is not able to be thought – which is extremely absurd. It is false, therefore, that something than which a greater is not able to be thought is not if it is able even to be thought – and more so, then, if it is able to be understood and to be in understanding.

I will say something more:[2] Beyond doubt, regarding anything that is not somewhere or at some time: even if it is somewhere or at some time, it is still able to be thought that it never is or that it is nowhere, just as it is not somewhere or is not at some time. For regarding something that was not yesterday and is today: just as it is understood that it was not yesterday, so it can be sub-understood never to be. And regarding something that is not here and is somewhere: just as it is not here, so it is able to be thought to be nowhere. Likewise regarding something of which there are individual parts: where or when there are other parts, all its parts – and so the whole itself – is able to be thought to be nowhere. For even if it is said that time always is and the world is everywhere, yet the former is not always as a whole nor is the latter everywhere as a whole. And just as individual parts of time are not when other parts are, so they are able to be thought never to be. And just as individual parts of the world are not where other parts are, so they are able to be sub-understood to be nowhere. But also, something that is joined together with parts is able in thought to be loosened apart and not to be. Hence, regarding anything that is not somewhere or at some time as a whole: even if it *is*, it is able to be thought not to be. Yet regarding that than which a greater is unable to be thought: if it *is*, it is not able to be thought not to be; otherwise, if it *is*, it is not that than which a greater is not able to be thought – which does not fit together. In no way, therefore, is it not somewhere or at some time as a whole; rather, it *is* as a whole always and everywhere.

Do you not deem that that about which these things are understood is able in some way to be thought or understood, or to be in thought or in understanding? For if it is not able, these things are not able to be understood concerning it. But if you say that that which is not thoroughly understood is not understood or is not in understanding, then tell me also that someone who is not able to gaze upon the purest light of the sun does not see the light of day, which is nothing except the light of the sun. Certainly in this way even that than which a greater cannot be thought is understood and is in understanding, so that these things are understood about it.

[II] And so in the argumentation that you reprehended, I said that when the fool hears "that than which a greater is not able to be thought" expressed, he understands what he hears. If it is said in a language with which he is familiar, then by all means the one who does not understand either has no understanding or has an understanding that has been buried over.

Then I said that if this expression is understood, it is in understanding. Is it that that which was shown to be in the truth of reality is necessarily in no understanding? But you will say that even if it is in understanding, it still does not follow that it is understood. But see this: it follows that it is in understanding from the fact that it is understood. For regarding that which is thought: it is thought in thought; and regarding that which is thought in thought: just as it is thought, so it is in thought. Likewise, regarding that which is understood: it is understood in understanding; and regarding that which is understood in understanding: just as it is understood, so it is in understanding. What is plainer than this?

After this I said that if it is even in understanding alone, it is able to be thought to be also in reality, which is greater. If, therefore, it is in understanding alone, that very thing – namely, that than which a greater is not able to be thought – is that than which a greater is able to be thought. I ask: What follows more? Is it that if it is even in understanding alone, it is not able to be thought to be also in reality? Or is it that if it is able to be thought to be also in reality, the one who thinks this thinks something greater than it, if it is in understanding alone? What, therefore, follows more than this: that if that than which a greater cannot be thought is in understanding alone, then that same thing is that than which a greater is able to be thought? But, by all means, in no understanding is that than which a greater is able to be thought the same as that than which a greater is not able to be thought. Is it, therefore, that this does not follow: that if that than which a greater cannot be thought is in any understanding, it is not in understanding alone? For if it is in understanding alone, it is that than which a greater is able to be thought – which does not fit together.

[III] But regarding an island in the ocean that surpasses all lands by its fruitfulness (which is named the "Lost Island" owing to the difficulty – or rather the impossibility – of finding that which is not): it is also the case, you say, that one might say that it is not able to be doubted that such an island truly is in reality, because one easily understands it when it is described in words. I say in all confidence that if someone were to find for me a thing that exists

either in reality itself or in thought alone (besides that than which a greater is
not able to be thought) to which one is able to apply readily the connection of
this argument of mine, I will find him and give him that Lost Island no more
to be lost! But clearly it is now seen that that than which a greater does not
avail to be thought is not able to be thought not to be, since it exists by this so
certain reason of truth. For otherwise it would exist in no way at all.

In sum, if someone says that he thinks that there is not something than
which a greater is not able to be thought, I say that when he is thinking this,
either he is thinking something than which a greater is not able to be thought
or he is not thinking it. If he is not thinking it, then he does not think that that
which he is not thinking is not. But if, in truth, he is thinking it, then by all
means he is thinking something that is not able to be thought not to be. For if
it were able to be thought not to be, it would be able to be thought to have a
beginning and an end. But this is not able to be. The one, therefore, who is
thinking that than which a greater is not able to be thought is thinking something that is not able to be thought not to be. In truth, the one who is thinking
this is not thinking that this very thing is not; otherwise, he is thinking that
which is not able to be thought. That than which a greater cannot be thought,
therefore, is not able to be thought not to be.

[IV] But, you say, when it is said that this abovemost reality cannot be
thought not to be, it would perhaps be better said that it is not able to be *understood* not to be, or even that it is not able to be *understood* not to be able not
to be. It was preferable, however, that it was said that it is not able to be *thought*
not to be. For if I had said that this reality is not able to be *understood* not to
be, perhaps you yourself who say these things would have objected that
(because false things cannot be *understood*, according to the proper meaning
of the word) nothing that *is* is able to be understood not to be. For it is false
that that which *is* is not. And on this account, it is not proper to God that he is
not able to be understood not to be. Because if any one of those things that
most certainly *are* are able to be understood not to be, likewise also other certain things are able to be understood not to be. But if one considers this well,
this objection is not able to be made concerning thought. For even if none of
the things that *are* are able to be *understood* not to be, yet all things are able
to be *thought* not to be – aside from that which *is* in the abovemost way.
Indeed, all and only those things that have a starting-point or an end or a joining together of parts, as well as anything (as I have already said) that is not
somewhere or at some time as a whole, are able to be thought not to be. In
truth, that alone in which there is no starting-point or end or joining together
of parts, and which no thought comes upon except as a whole always and
everywhere – that alone is not able to be thought not to be.[3]

Know, therefore, that you are able to think that you are not even while you
know most certainly that you are. I marvel that you said that you did not know

this. For we think many things not to be that we know to be and many things to be that we know not to be – not by judging it to be such as we think it, but by fashioning it thus. And, indeed, we are able to think something not to be even when we know it to be, since at once we are able to think the former and know the latter. And we are not able to think that something is not when we know it to be, because we are not able to think at once that it is and that it is not. If, therefore, someone were to distinguish two senses of this statement in this way, he would understand that (in one sense) nothing is able to be thought not to be when it is known that it *is* and that (in another sense) anything that *is* – aside from that than which a greater cannot be thought – is able to be thought not to be. So, therefore, it is proper to God that he is not able to be thought not to be, and many things are able to be thought not to be even when they *are*. And in what manner it may be said that God is thought not to be was, I deem, spoken of sufficiently in that little book.

[V] It is easy, even for one who is a little wise, to counter these and other things that you object to me on behalf of the fool, and for this reason I had judged that I should refrain from showing this. But because I am hearing that it seems to some who read your objections that they avail somewhat against me, I will recall a few of them.

First, you often repeat that I say the following: that which is greater than all things is in understanding; if it is in understanding, it is also in reality; for otherwise that which is greater than all things would not be greater than all things. Nowhere in the things said by me is that proof found. For saying "greater than all things" and saying "that than which a greater cannot be thought" do not avail in the same way toward proving that what is said is also in reality. For if someone were to say that that than which a greater is not able to be thought is not something in reality, or that it is able not to be, or even that it is able to be thought not to be, he is able to be refuted easily. For that which is not, is able not to be; and that which is able not to be, is able to be thought not to be. But regarding anything that is able to be thought not to be: if it *is*, it is not that than which a greater is not able to be thought; and if it is not, then even if it might be, by all means it would not be that than which a greater is not able to be thought. But regarding that than which a greater is not able to be thought: it is not able to be said that if it *is*, it is not that than which a greater is not able to be thought; nor is it able to be said that if it is not but might be, it would not be that than which a greater is not able to be thought. It is clear, then, that it is not the case that it is not, nor that it is able not to be, nor that it is it able to be thought not to be. For otherwise, if it *is*, it is not that which it is said to be; and if it is not but might be, it would not be that which it is said to be.

But this does not seem able to be proved so easily concerning that which is said to be "greater than all things." For the claim "that which is able to be thought not to be is not greater than all things that are" is not as clear as the claim "that which is able to be thought not to be is not that than which a greater is not able to be thought." Nor is it so indubitable that if there is something greater than all things, it is not something other than that than which a greater is not able to be thought; nor is it so indubitable that if it were something other, it would not *be* in a similar way, namely, in that certain manner that belongs to that which is said to be "that than which a greater cannot be thought." For what if someone were to say that there is something greater than all things that are, and yet it itself is able to be thought not to be? And what if he were to say also that something greater than it, even though it is not, is yet able to be thought? And regarding the latter [i.e., something able to be thought that is greater than that which is greater than all things], isn't it the case that it can be inferred just as manifestly, then, that it is not greater than all the things that are; just as it may be said most manifestly regarding the former [i.e., that which is greater than all things] that it is not, then, that than which a greater cannot be thought? For in the case of "that which is greater than all things," an argument other than that it is said to be greater than all things is needed, whereas in the case I laid out there is no need for anything other than this very thing that one announces, "that than which a greater is not able to be thought." If, then, what that than which a greater cannot be thought proves about itself in its own right is not able to be proved likewise about that which is said to be greater than all things, then you have reprehended me unjustly for having said something that I did not say, since it differs so much from what I did say.

And yet, in truth, if it is able to be proved after another argument, you ought not to have reprehended me in this way for having said that it is able to be proved. One who recognizes that that than which a greater cannot be thought is able to be greater than all things easily assesses whether it is able to be proved. For in no way is that than which a greater is not able to be thought able to be understood except as that alone which is greater than all things. Just as, therefore, that than which a greater cannot be thought is understood and is in understanding, and so also it is asserted to be in the truth of reality; so, too, that which is said to be greater than all things is understood and is in understanding, and on this account it is concluded of necessity to be in reality itself. Do you see, then, how rightly you compared me to that dullard who willed to assert that the Lost Island *is* merely on the grounds that the things described were understood?

[VI] Now, you object that any false or doubtful things whatsoever are able to be understood and to be in understanding in that manner in which that about which I was speaking is able. I wonder what you perceived in this objection against me, who wanted to prove something doubtful and for whom it was enough at first that I show it to be understood and to be in understanding in any manner whatsoever, so long as one considers subsequently whether it is able to be in understanding alone, as false things are, or also in reality, as true things are. For if false and doubtful things are understood and are in understanding in this manner – namely, that when they are said, the one hearing understands what the one speaking is signifying – nothing forbids it from being said that they are understood and are in understanding. In what manner, however, do the things you say fit together with each other: that when someone speaks, you would understand any of the false things he would say; and that regarding that which is in thought not in that manner in which even false things are, you would not say that you are thinking it or that you have it in thought when it is heard, but rather that you understand it and have it in understanding, because otherwise you would not be able to think it without understanding it, that is, without comprehending by knowledge that it exists in reality itself? In what manner, I say, do these fit together: that false things are understood, and that to understand is to comprehend by knowledge that something exists? Do you see that there is nothing against me here? Rather, if false things are understood in some manner, and if the aforesaid definition of understanding is a definition not of every understanding, but only of some: then you ought not to have reprehended me because I said that that than which a greater is not able to be thought is understood and is in understanding even before it was certain that it exists in reality itself.

[VII] Next, you say that it is hardly able even to be believed that when this has been said or heard, it is not able to be thought not to be in that manner in which even God is not able to be thought not to be. Those who have attained even a slight knowledge of disputing and arguing may respond to this on my behalf. For is it reasonable that someone deny something that he understands on account of the fact that it is said to be that which he denies because he does not understand it? Or if that which is understood in some way is denied sometimes, and it is the same thing as that which is understood in no way: isn't it proved more easily that there is doubt about its being in some understanding than that there is doubt about its being in no understanding at all? In what way is it able to be believed that anyone denies that he understands that than which a greater cannot be thought in some way when it has been heard because he denies God, the meaning of whom he is thinking in no manner at all? Or even if that than which a greater cannot be thought is denied because it is not altogether understood: isn't this proved more easily regarding that which is understood in no manner at all than regarding that which is understood in some manner? Not unreasonably, then, did I bring to bear that than which a greater cannot be thought against the fool in order to prove that there is a God, because he understands God in no manner at all, whereas in some manner he does understand that than which a greater is not able to be thought.

[VIII] It is without cause that you so eagerly prove that that than which a greater cannot be thought is not of the same sort as a picture in a painter's understanding that has not yet been made. For I did not bring forward a picture that is thought out beforehand because I wanted to assert it as something of the same sort as that which I was treating, but only because I was able to show it as something that is in understanding which may be understood not to be.

Again, you say that when that than which a greater cannot be thought is heard by you, you are not able to think it or hold it in understanding in relation to a reality of which you are aware either from its genus or from its species, because neither are you aware of the reality itself nor are you able to conjecture it from another reality like it. Clearly, however, the reality of the situation is otherwise. For since every lesser good is similar to a greater good inasmuch as it is good, it is clear to any reasonable mind whatsoever that – because by a gathering ascent[4] from lesser goods to greater ones something greater is able to be thought from them – we are very much able to conjecture that than which nothing greater is able to be thought. Who, for example, is not able to think at least this – even if he does not believe that that which he is thinking is in reality – namely, that if there is something good that has a starting-point and an end, then better by much more is a good that, although it begins, does not cease to be? And just as the latter is better than the former, so also that which has neither an end nor a starting-point is better than the latter, even if it is always passing from the past through the present toward the future. And still better than this is that which in no manner needs to change or to move or is compelled to do so – whether something of this sort is in reality or not. Is it that this is not able to be thought or that something greater than this is able to be thought? Or is it that one is not conjecturing that than which a greater cannot be thought from those things than which a greater avails to be thought? It is from this, therefore, that one is able to conjecture that than which a greater cannot be thought. And so in this way the fool who does not accept sacred authority can be refuted easily if he denies that that than which a greater does not avail to be thought is able to be conjectured from other things. And if some Catholic Christian were to deny this, he should remember that the invisible things of God are seen, being understood through the things that have been made – even his everlasting power and divinity.[5]

[IX] If it were true, however, that that than which a greater cannot be thought is not able to be thought or understood, it would still not be false that that than which a greater cannot be thought is able to be thought or understood. For just as no one forbids that "ineffable" be said, although that which is said to be ineffable cannot be said; and just as "unthinkable" is able to be thought, even though that with which "unthinkable" fits is not able be thought; so when "that than which nothing greater avails to be thought" is said, beyond doubt that which is heard is able to be thought and understood, even if that reality than which a greater cannot be thought does not avail to be thought or understood. For even if someone is such a fool as to say that there is not something than which a greater is not able to be thought, he will nonetheless not be so shameless as to say that he is not able to understand or think that which he says. Or if someone is found to be so shameless, not only is his word to be rejected, but he himself should be rejected along with it. And certainly, therefore, whoever denies that there is something than which a greater cannot be thought understands and thinks the denial that he makes. He is not able to understand or think this denial without its parts. But part of it is "that than which a greater is not able to be thought." Whoever denies this, therefore, understands and thinks that than which a greater cannot be thought. But clearly it is the case that that which is not able not to be is able likewise to be thought and understood. In truth, the one who is thinking this is thinking something greater than the one who is thinking that which is able not to be. When, therefore, that than which a greater is not able to be thought is thought, if it is thought that it is able not to be, then that than which a greater is not able to be thought is not being thought. But the same thing cannot both be thought and not be thought simultaneously. Therefore, the one who is thinking that than which a greater is not able to be thought is not thinking that it is able not to be, but that it is not able not to be. On account of this, it is necessary that that which he is thinking *is*, because whatever is able not to be is not that which he is thinking.

[X] I deem that I have shown that in the aforesaid little book I have proved, not by weak argumentation, but by sufficiently necessary argumentation, that there exists in reality itself something than which a greater is not able to be thought. Nor do I deem that this argumentation is weakened by the strength of any objection. For the signification of this expression contains in itself so much power that this very thing that is said, by the very fact that it is understood and thought, is proved of necessity both to exist in true reality and itself to be anything whatever it behooves us to believe about the divine substance. For about the divine substance, we believe it to be anything whatever that without qualification is able to be thought better to be than not to be. It is better, for example, to be eternal than not to be eternal, to be good than not to be good – or rather to be goodness itself than not to be goodness itself. But that than which something greater is not able to be thought is not able to be none of these things. It is necessary, therefore, that that than which a greater is not able to be thought is whatever it behooves one to believe about the divine substance.

I thank you for your being well-disposed in both your reprehending and your praise of my little work. For it was with great praise that you extolled those things that seemed to you worthy of acceptance. And it is apparent enough that with goodwill, not ill-will, you reprehended those things that seemed to you weak.

Appendix 1: *Monologion*, Prologue

Certain brothers often and eagerly entreated me that I write out for them, as a model of a meditation, certain things I brought up in everyday discussions about meditating on the essence of divinity, as well as other such things consistent with a meditation of this sort. For my writing this meditation, moreover, they determined in advance – more in accord with their own wish than with the ease of the thing or my ability – the following form: that nothing at all in it should be urged by the authority of Scripture; rather, in a plain style and by common arguments and simple disputation, whatever the conclusion should assert through the individual investigations, both the necessity of reason should compel briefly and the clarity of truth should show openly. They also wished that I not disdain to meet with simple and almost foolish objections that occur to me.

Indeed, for a while I refused to attempt this and, comparing myself with this task, I tried to excuse myself by many arguments. For the more they wanted what they asked for to be easily of use to themselves, the more difficult it was to accomplish what they enjoined upon me. At length, however, overcome with the modest forcefulness of their entreaties and not disdaining the honesty of their eagerness, I began the task they entreated, though with reluctance on account of the difficulty of the thing and the feebleness of my mind; yet, on account of their charity, I carried it out with pleasure as much as I was able to do in accord with their terms. I was led to do so with the hope that whatever I did would be known only to those who had demanded it and that a little while later it would be buried in contempt by these same brothers, who would scorn it as something worthless. For in this task I know that I was not so much able to satisfy those entreating me as I was able to put an end to the entreaties that were pursuing me. But I do not know by what means it came about against my hope that not only the aforesaid brothers, but also many others busied themselves in commending this very writing to long memory by making copies for themselves.

Going back over this writing often, I was able to find nothing I said in it that is not consistent with the writings of the catholic Fathers, and especially those of blessed Augustine. Thus if it will seem to someone that in this same small work I have put forth something that either is exceedingly novel or dissents from the truth, I ask – lest he immediately call me either a presumer of novelties or an assertor of falsity – that he look diligently beforehand at the books of the aforementioned Augustine's *On the Trinity*. For when I said that the abovemost Trinity can be said to be three substances, I followed the Greeks, who confess three substances in one person by the same faith by which we confess three persons in one substance. For by "substance" they signify in God that which we signify by "person." But whatever things I said there were spoken under the person of one arguing and investigating with himself by thought alone things to which he had not paid attention before, just as I knew was wanted by those whose petitioning I aimed to heed.

Now, I entreat and beg vehemently that if someone wants to copy this small work, he take care to put this preface at the head of the little book before the chapters themselves. For I think that it would be of much profit toward understanding the things which one reads here if beforehand someone knew with what intention or in what manner they were argued. I also think that if someone sees this preface beforehand, he will not judge rashly if he were to find something put forth against his own opinion.

Appendix 2: Keys to translated words

The following keys are in no way all-inclusive, but they do include many of the prominent Latin words in Anselm's original *Proslogion* and their English renderings in this translation. For the most part I have rendered the same Latin word consistently with the corresponding English word. The first list provides the original Latin words in alphabetical order, while the second provides the English renderings in alphabetical order. In both lists I have indicated the part of speech that the English rendering takes.

Latin	English
absens	absent (adj.)
accedere	approach (v.)
acies	focus (n.)
acuere	focus (v.)
adversare	turn against (v.)
aestimare	reckon (v.)
affectare	long (v.)
affectus	affect (n.)
afficeri	be affected (v.)
alienus	foreign (adj.)
aliquatenus	to some extent (adv.)
amplitudo	ampleness (n.)
amplus	ample (adj.)
angustia	narrowness (n.)
anima	soul (n.)
argumentum	argument (n.)
aspicere	look at (v.)
astruere	build toward (v.)
auscultare	listen (v.)
beatus	blessed (adj.)
bene	well (adv.)
benignus	well-disposed (adj.)
bonus	good (adj.)
bonitas	goodness (n.)
capere	grasp (v.)

carere	lack (v.)
cernere	discern (v.)
cerneri	be discerned (v.)
certe	certainly (adv.)
certitudo	certainty (n.)
certus	certain (adj.)
circumspicere	look around (v.)
claudere	enclose (v.)
clausus	closed (adj.)
clementia	clemency (n.)
coercere	constrain (v.)
cognoscere	recognize (v.)
conare	endeavor (v.)
concordare	accord with (v.)
coniectatio	conjecturing (n.)
conicere	conjecture (v.)
contrahere	constrict (v.)
convertere	turn back (v.)
cogitatio	thought (n.)
comitare	accompany (v.)
compassio	suffering with another (n.)
contemplare	contemplate (v.)
cor	heart (n.)
credere	believe (v.)
cupere	yearn (v.)
damnare	condemn (v.)
delectabilis	delightful (adj.)
delectatio	delight (n.)
desiderare	desire (v.)
desinere	cease (v.)
desperare	despair (v.)
dicere	say; speak (v.)
dirus	horrible (adj.)
docere	teach (v.)
durus	hard (adj.)
effectus	effect (n.)
egere	be in need (v.)
egestas	neediness (n.)
eia	quick (interj.)
elongatus	removed far from (adj.)
erigere	straighten up (v.)
esurire	hunger (v.)

excedere	exceed (v.)
excitare	rouse (v.)
excitatio	rousing (n.)
exemplum	model (n.)
expedire	be advantageous (v.)
facies	face (n.)
fas	permissible (adj.)
feliciter	happily (adv.)
felix	happy (adj.)
fides	faith (n.)
fluvius	river (n.)
flumen	stream (n.)
fons	spring (n.)
gaudium	joy (n.)
ignorare	be unfamiliar (v.)
illuminare	enlighten (v.)
immensitas	unmeasuredness (n.)
immensus	unmeasured (adj.)
impotens	unable (adj.)
impotentia	inability (n.)
inaccessibilis	unapproachable (adj.)
inchoare	start (v.)
incipere	begin (v.)
incircumscriptus	uncircumscribed (adj.)
infirmus	sick (adj.)
influere	flow into (v.)
inhabitare	dwell in (v.)
initium	starting-point (n.)
insipiens	fool (n.)
intellectus	understanding (n.)
intendere	stretch toward/out (v.)
interminabile	unboundable (adj.)
intimus	inmost (adj.)
intuitus	gaze (n.)
intus	interiorly (adv.)
invenire	come upon (v.)
inveniri	be come upon (v.)
investigare	track down (v.)
iucunditas	pleasantness (n.)
iucundus	pleasant (adj.)
iudicare	judge (v.)
iustitia	justice (n.)

iustus	just (adj.)
laetitia	gladness (n.)
languor	weariness (n.)
latere	hide (v.)
lex	law (n.)
liberare	set free (v.)
locus	place (n.)
luctus	grief (n.)
magis	more (adv.)
maius	greater (adj.)
malus	evil (adj.)
meditare	meditate (v.)
meditatio	meditation (n.)
melius	better (adj.)
mens	mind (n.)
meritum	merited, merit (adj., n.)
micare	glimmer (v.)
minus	less (adv.)
mirari	be wondered at (v.)
mirum	wonder (n.)
miserabilis	pitiable (adj.)
miserare	pity (v.)
misere	pitifully (adv.)
miseria	pitifulness (n.)
misericordia	pity-heartedness (n.)
misericors	pity-hearted (adj.)
miserus	pitiful (adj.)
modus	manner (n.)
mutatio	change (n.)
nasci	be born (v.)
nefas	impermissible (adj.)
nequire	cannot (v.)
nescire	not know (v.)
noscere	be aware of (v.)
nolere	will against (v.)
obrigescere	stiffen (v.)
obruere	overwhelm, bury over (v.)
obscurare	obscure (v.)
obstruere	be blocked up (v.)
obstupescere	become dull (v.)
oculus	eye (n.)
opinari	opine (v.)

ostendere	show (v.)
parcere	spare (v.)
penetrare	penetrate (v.)
penitus	thoroughly (adv.)
persona	person (n.)
perspiceri	be perceived all through (v.)
pervidere	see all through (v.)
pervideri	be seen all through (v.)
plus	more (adv.)
pius	kind (adj.)
posse	be able (v.)
postulare	demand (v.)
potens	able (adj.)
potentia	ability (n.)
praesens	present (adj.)
principium	beginning (n.)
procedere	proceed (v.)
profluere	flow forth (v.)
proiectus	cast forth (adj.)
publicus	common (adj.)
pure	purely (adv.)
quaerere	seek (v.)
quomodo	in what manner (adv.)
ratio	reason (n.)
requirere	seek again (v.)
repugnantia	contrariety (n.)
repugnare	counteract (v.)
res	reality (n.)
restituere	restore (v.)
retribuere	pay back (v.)
reverberare	beat back (v.)
reus	guilty (adj.)
sapere	wisely know (v.)
sapientia	wisdom (n.)
satietas	satedness (n.)
saturitas	satiety (n.)
simplicitas	simplicity (n.)
simul	simultaneously (adv.)
sperare	hope (v.)
splendor	splendor (n.)
sponte	voluntarily (adv.)
stultus	dull (adj.)

subintelligi	be sub-understood (v.)
summus	abovemost (adj.)
suspirare	sigh (v.)
tempus	time (n.)
tenebrare	darkness (n.)
tenebrae	darken (v.)
turbatio	trouble (n.)
ulcisci	avenge (v.)
unde	from where/which (adv.)
valere	avail (v.)
verax	truthful (adj.)
vere	truly (adv.)
veritas	truth (n.)
versari	move about (v.)
verum	in truth (adv.)
verus	true (adj.)
vetustus	ancient (adj.)
videre	see (v.)
vincere	conquer (v.)
vita	life (n.)
vivere	live (v.)
vultus	countenance (n.)

English	Latin
ability (n.)	*potentia*
able (adj.)	*potens*
abovemost (adj.)	*summus*
absent (adj.)	*absens*
accompany (v.)	*comitare*
accord with (v.)	*concordare*
affect (n.)	*affectus*
ample (adj.)	*amplus*
ampleness (n.)	*amplitudo*
ancient (adj.)	*vetustus*
approach (v.)	*accedere*
argument (n.)	*argumentum*
avail (v.)	*valere*
avenge (v.)	*ulcisci*
be able (v.)	*posse*
be advantageous (v.)	*expedire*
be affected (v.)	*afficeri*
be aware of (v.)	*noscere*

be blocked up (v.)	obstruere
be born (v.)	nasci
be come upon (v.)	inveniri
be discerned (v.)	cerneri
be in need (v.)	egere
be perceived all through (v.)	perspiceri
be seen all through (v.)	pervideri
be sub-understood (v.)	subintelligi
be unfamiliar (v.)	*ignorare*
be wondered at (v.)	mirari
beat back (v.)	reverberare
become dull (v.)	obstupescere
begin (v.)	incipere
beginning (n.)	principium
believe (v.)	credere
better (adj.)	melius
blessed (adj.)	beatus
build toward (v.)	astruere
bury over (v.)	obruere
cannot (v.)	nequire
cast forth (adj.)	proiectus
cease (v.)	desinere
certain (adj.)	certus
certainly (adv.)	certe
certainty (n.)	certitudo
change (n.)	mutatio
clemency (n.)	clementia
closed (adj.)	clausus
come upon (v.)	invenire
common (adj.)	publicus
condemn (v.)	damnare
conjecture (v.)	conicere
conjecturing (n.)	coniectatio
conquer (v.)	vincere
constrain (v.)	coercere
constrict (v.)	contrahere
contemplate (v.)	contemplare
contrariety (n.)	repugnantia
countenance (n.)	vultus
counteract (v.)	repugnare
darken (v.)	tenebrare
darkness (n.)	tenebrae

delight (n.)	*delectatio*
delightful (adj.)	*delectabilis*
demand (v.)	*postulare*
desire (v.)	*desiderare*
despair (v.)	*desperare*
discern (v.)	*cernere*
dull (adj.)	*stultus*
dwell in (v.)	*inhabitare*
effect (n.)	*effectus*
enclose (v.)	*claudere*
endeavor (v.)	*conare*
enlighten (v.)	*illuminare*
evil (adj.)	*malus*
exceed (v.)	*excedere*
eye (n.)	*oculus*
face (n.)	*facies*
faith (n.)	*fides*
flow forth (v.)	*profluere*
flow into (v.)	*influere*
focus (n.)	*acies*
focus (v.)	*acuere*
fool (n.)	*insipiens*
foreign (adj.)	*alienus*
from where (adv.)	*unde*
from which (adv.)	*unde*
gaze (n.)	*intuitus*
gladness (n.)	*laetitia*
glimmer (v.)	*micare*
good (adj.)	*bonus*
goodness (n.)	*bonitas*
grasp (v.)	*capere*
greater (adj.)	*maius*
grief (n.)	*luctus*
guilty (adj.)	*reus*
happily (adv.)	*feliciter*
happy (adj.)	*felix*
hard (adj.)	*durus*
heart (n.)	*cor*
hide (v.)	*latere*
hope (v.)	*sperare*
horrible (adj.)	*dirus*
hunger (v.)	*esurire*

impermissible (adj.)	*nefas*
in truth (adv.)	*verum*
in what manner (adv.)	*quomodo*
inability (n.)	*impotentia*
inmost (adj.)	*intimus*
interiorly (adv.)	*intus*
joy (n.)	*gaudium*
judge (v.)	*iudicare*
just (adj.)	*iustus*
justice (n.)	*iustitia*
kind (adj.)	*pius*
lack (v.)	*carere*
law (n.)	*lex*
less (adv.)	*minus*
life (n.)	*vita*
listen (v.)	*auscultare*
live (v.)	*vivere*
long (v.)	*affectare*
look around (v.)	*circumspicere*
look at (v.)	*aspicere*
manner (n.)	*modus*
meditate (v.)	*meditare*
meditation (n.)	*meditatio*
merit (n.)	*meritum*
merited (adj.)	*meritum*
mind (n.)	*mens*
model (n.)	*exemplum*
more (adv.)	*magis*
more (adv.)	*plus*
move about (v.)	*versari*
narrowness (n.)	*angustia*
neediness (n.)	*egestas*
not know (v.)	*nescire*
obscure (v.)	*obscurare*
opine (v.)	*opinari*
overwhelm (v.)	*obruere*
pay back (v.)	*retribuere*
penetrate (v.)	*penetrare*
permissible (adj.)	*fas*
person (n.)	*persona*
pitiable (adj.)	*miserabilis*
pitiful (adj.)	*miserus*

pitifully (adv.)	*misere*
pitifulness (n.)	*miseria*
pity (v.)	*miserare*
pity-hearted (adj.)	*misericors*
pity-heartedness (n.)	*misericordia*
place (n.)	*locus*
pleasant (adj.)	*iucundus*
pleasantness (n.)	*iucunditas*
present (adj.)	*praesens*
proceed (v.)	*procedere*
purely (adv.)	*pure*
quick (interj.)	*eia*
reality (n.)	*res*
reason (n.)	*ratio*
reckon (v.)	*aestimare*
recognize (v.)	*cognoscere*
removed far from (adj.)	*elongatus*
restore (v.)	*restituere*
river (n.)	*fluvius*
rouse (v.)	*excitare*
rousing (n.)	*excitatio*
satedness (n.)	*satietas*
satiety (n.)	*saturitas*
say (v.)	*dicere*
see (v.)	*videre*
see all through (v.)	*pervidere*
seek (v.)	*quaerere*
seek again (v.)	*requirere*
set free (v.)	*liberare*
show (v.)	*ostendere*
sick (adj.)	*infirmus*
sigh (v.)	*suspirare*
simplicity (n.)	*simplicitas*
simultaneously (adv.)	*simul*
soul (n.)	*anima*
spare (v.)	*parcere*
speak (v.)	*dicere*
splendor (n.)	*splendor*
spring (n.)	*fons*
start (v.)	*inchoare*
starting-point (n.)	*initium*
stiffen (v.)	*obrigescere*

straighten up (v.)	*erigere*
stream (n.)	*flumen*
stretch out (v.)	*intendere*
stretch toward (v.)	*intendere*
suffering with another (n.)	*compassio*
teach (v.)	*docere*
thoroughly (adv.)	*penitus*
thought (n.)	*cogitatio*
time (n.)	*tempus*
to some extent (adv.)	*aliquatenus*
track down (v.)	*investigare*
trouble (n.)	*turbatio*
true (adj.)	*verus*
truly (adv.)	*vere*
truth (n.)	*veritas*
truthful (adj.)	*verax*
turn against (v.)	*adversare*
turn back (v.)	*convertere*
unable (adj.)	*impotens*
unapproachable (adj.)	*inaccessibilis*
unboundable (adj.)	*interminabile*
uncircumscribed (adj.)	*incircumscriptus*
understanding (n.)	*intellectus*
unmeasured (adj.)	*immensus*
unmeasuredness (n.)	*immensitas*
voluntarily (adv.)	*sponte*
weariness (n.)	*languor*
well (adv.)	*bene*
well-disposed (adj.)	*benignus*
will against (v.)	*nolere*
wisdom (n.)	*sapientia*
wisely know (v.)	*sapere*
wonder (n.)	*mirum*
yearn (v.)	*cupere*

Endnotes

Introduction

1   *Vita S. Benedicti (ex libro II Dialogorum S. Gregorii Magni excerpta)*, xxxv (PL 66, 198A-B).

2   *Vita S. Benedicti*, cxxxv (PL 66, 200A-B).

3   *Vita S. Benedicti*, prol. (PL 66, 126A).

4   For more on this, see J. Leclercq, *The Love of Learning and the Desire for God: A Study of Monastic Culture*, trans. C. Misrahi (New York: Fordham University Press, 1982).

5   Such details, as well as those relating to the rest of Anselm's life, can be found in Eadmer's *Vita Anselmi*, a biography written by Anselm's friend and brother monk. See Eadmer, *The Life of St. Anselm, Archbishop of Canterbury*, trans. R. Southern (Oxford: Oxford University Press, 1962). This edition includes both the Latin text and an English translation of the *Vita Anselmi*. In addition to translating Eadmer's account of Anselm's life, Southern has also written a magisterial biography of Anselm: *Saint Anselm: A Portrait in a Landscape* (Cambridge: Cambridge University Press, 1990). The dates for the works that I indicate in this Introduction are based on this work.

6   Eadmer, *Vita Anselmi*, 29–30 (my translation).

7   For more on the significance of Chapter 1 in relation to the *Proslogion* as a whole, see my M. Walz, "The 'Logic' of Faith Seeking Understanding: A Propaedeutic for Anselm's *Proslogion*," *Dionysius* 28 (2010): 131–66.

8   It does not seem accidental that at the conclusion of the Preface of the *Proslogion*, Anselm interprets or translates the title of his previous work, *Monologion* (a word with Greek roots), as *soliloquium*, a Latin word. Certainly Anselm intends to call our attention to Augustine's *Soliloquies* when he does so.

9   *Soliloquiorum libri duo*, I.vi.13 (PL 32, 876).

10   *De ordine libri duo*, II.xi.30 (PL 32, 1009).

11   For more on this, see M. Walz, "An Erotic Pattern of Thinking in Anselm's *Proslogion*," *Quaestiones Disputatae* 2 (2011): 126–45.

12   192a–193a.

13   Elizabeth Barrett Browning captures the parameters of such *eros* beautifully in the opening lines of her well-known Sonnet 43:

> How do I love thee? Let me count the ways.
> I love thee to the depth and breadth and height
> My soul can reach, when feeling out of sight
> For the ends of being and ideal grace

Preface

1   Anselm is referring to the *Monologion*, whose Preface is included here as an
     appendix so that the reader can compare its stated goals and method to those of
     the *Proslogion*.

2   "Abovemost" renders the adjective *summus*. *Summus* is a shortened version of
     supremus, the superlative form of *super* ("over" or "above"). It is usually rendered
     "highest" or "supreme," but I render it "abovemost" in order to emphasize how
     this adjective suggests being superlative with regard to an already comparative
     relationship of "height," broadly conceived. To be *summus* is, as it were, to be
     "higher-est." To be "abovemost," then, may involve not only being what is "high-
     est" or "supreme" within a given range; in addition, it may involve standing in
     relation to any range as beyond or above it – and thus, perhaps, standing as the
     intelligible ground of there being any such hierarchical ranges whatsoever.

3   Anselm outlines the *Proslogion* as a whole according to three "tasks" or "goals,"
     namely, building toward [*astruendum*] (1) that God truly is, (2) that God is the
     abovemost good who needs no other, and (3) that God is the abovemost good
     whom all other things need in order both to be and to be well. (Anselm adds a
     fourth or, as I think, an overall task, namely, building toward whatever we believe
     about the divine substance.) These three tasks may be seen as corresponding with
     three "thoughts" or articulations of God that Anselm introduces along the way:
     "something than which nothing greater is able to be thought" (Chapter 2), "some-
     thing greater than is able to be thought" (Chapter 15), and "that [delightful] good
     . . . which contains the pleasantness of all goods" (Chapter 24). From the start,
     then, Anselm suggests a tripartite structure of the work and thus encourages the
     reader to begin "thinking in threes."

4   "My mind's focus" renders *mentis acies*, a phrase one sometimes encounters in
     Augustine's writings when he refers to the human cognitive capacity to apprehend
     higher, necessary truths, i.e., truths that bear on spiritual or immaterial realities.
     More literally, *acies* refers to a sharp point or edge. Speaking of the *acies mentis*,
     then, suggests a mind looking upward and reaching a unifying focal point where-
     by it "sees" or has insight into a spiritual reality (including, it appears, even the
     mind's insight into itself as immaterial). Anselm's description here indicates, then,
     that the reality of God is ever escaping this focal point that the mind's eye reach-
     es; God always flees beyond the reach of the mind's capacity of upward looking.
     As we see just below, however, a thought eventually offers itself to Anselm where-
     by the reality of God somehow comes into better focus for him, although the artic-
     ulation of that thought in Chapter 2 ("something than which nothing greater is able
     to be thought") still indicates that God ever surpasses the reach of the mind's eye.

5   The Latin here is: . . . *ab inquisitione rei quam inveniri esset impossibile*. The ren-
     dering in English is a bit awkward: ". . . from my searching for a reality that can-
     not possibly be come upon." The feature in question (i.e., the impossibility of
     being come upon) belongs to the reality for which Anselm is searching. This pas-
     sage suggests, then, that not being able to come upon this reality is owing not so
     much to the limited cognitive powers of human beings as to that reality's "inabil-
     ity" to be found. The reality in question, of course, is God, and so Anselm may be
     suggesting the hiddenness of God, a hiddenness that bespeaks something about the

Creator and not simply the limitations of creatures. Perhaps one could say that God is *essentially* hidden or perhaps even "hiddenness itself." Of course, any attempt to articulate such a hidden divine reality, as Anselm does in this work, introduces a unique set of difficulties.

6 The *cogitatio* ("thought") in question *se obtulit* ("offers itself"); it is *received*, not achieved, by Anselm. Hence the central thought that energizes the *Proslogion* is accepted by Anselm as a gift, a self-offering of the reality signified by that thought. In his reply to Gaunilo, Anselm does suggest a way of conjecturing this thought "philosophically," so to speak (see Anselm's Reply, [VIII]). Nonetheless, it is important to recognize that Anselm's thought of God is originally given to him as a gift, and in writing the *Proslogion* he in turn passes this gift on to the reader so that (as he puts it just below) "what [he] was pleased to have come upon would be pleasing to someone reading it."

7 These original and more descriptive titles of the *Monologion* and *Proslogion* distinguish them from one another and illuminate the character of each. The *Monologion* is an *exemplum*, a model or pattern, of the activity of meditating about the "reason of faith." It is a model, in other words, of the inquisitive movement according to which the complex intelligibility of faith is unfolded. The *Proslogion*, on the other hand, is not an *exemplum* ("model"); rather, it embodies an activity, namely, the activity of *fides quaerens intellectum*, "faith seeking understanding" or "trust striving after insight." It recapitulates Anselm's activity of believing insofar as it involves an innate inquisitive movement toward insight into what it already thinks with assent. More particularly, the *Proslogion* appears to recapitulate for the reader the very event that Anselm describes in the Preface, which resulted in a thought offering itself to him so that he could achieve greater insight into the reality of God.

8 Anselm ends the Preface by offering Latin equivalents to the familiar Greek-based titles. Thereby he calls attention to the fact that the former work was a "speaking alone" (*soliloquium*), while the present work is a "speaking to" someone (*allocutio*). The *Proslogion* fulfills this latter description primarily inasmuch as it is written in the form of a prayer to God and secondarily inasmuch as it is an exhortation to the reader to participate in Anselm's own prayer to (or contemplation of) God, i.e., his raising of his heart and mind to God.

Chapters

1 Psalms 13:1; 52:1.
2 Psalm 24:10.
3 Psalm 144:17.
4 I Tim. 6:16.

Proslogion

1 "Rousing" renders *excitatio*, a noun that can refer both to getting someone excited by means of rhetoric and to waking someone up. "Rousing" captures both meanings at once. (More literally, *excitatio* might be rendered "quickening.") It is noteworthy, I think, that Augustine uses the verb *excitare* three times in Book VIII of the *Confessions*, the book in which he describes the final stages of his conver-

sion to Christianity. Each use, I think, sheds light on the character of the *Proslogion*. See *Confessions*, VIII.4.9, VIII.7.17, and VIII.8.19. The third use, in fact, alludes to Matthew 6:6, just as Anselm does here in the opening line of this chapter.

In Chapter 1, it is possible to identify "phases" of this rousing; in fact, these phases correspond roughly with the paragraph breaks in the translated text. It would be too much to recount them here. For more on this, see M. Walz, "The 'Logic' of Faith Seeking Understanding: A Propaedeutic for Anselm's *Proslogion*," *Dionysius* 28 (2010): 131–66.

2   Matthew 6:6.

3   Psalm 26:8.

4   I Timothy 6:16.

5   This question sets the tone for the work. To approach God by means of a sign or face is to approach God indirectly. It is to get at God from the "outside," so to speak, by considering the way God "interfaces" with reality while remaining beyond it. But what can serve as an adequate sign or face of God for us human seekers? This question hovers over the opening chapter until its concluding lines and the opening lines of Chapter 2, where Anselm offers the reader the "intelligible face" of God in the very thinking of "something than which nothing greater is able to be thought" by a creature who has the image of God.

6   Psalm 50:13.

7   There are three verbs in this sentence, two of which are the same: *factus sum* ("I was made"), *feci* ("have I made"), *factus sum* ("I was made"). Each is a form of *facere*, "to make" or "to do." The second, *feci*, could be rendered here more colloquially as "have I done," but retaining the root connection between the verbs in English seems more important in this context, inasmuch as it indicates the human being's possible cooperation with the intention of his Maker by an act of human "making" or "doing."

8   Psalm 77:25.

9   Psalm 126:2.

10 Psalm 121:9.

11 Jeremiah 14:19.

12 Psalm 114:3.

13 Psalm 37:9.

14 Psalm 6:4.

15 Psalm 12:1.

16 Psalm 12:4.

17 Psalm 79:4.

18 This sentence subtly suggests an important "intelligible structure" of human existence. Things can be going either well or ill for a human being. In the former case, it is owing to the presence or activity of God, who gives us more than we are by nature ("*well*-being") inasmuch as he "gifts" or graces us; in the latter case, it is owing to our sinning, whereby we fail to live up to what we are made to be by nature ("*ill*-being") by rendering back to God less than he deserves. Well-being and ill-being "mirror" each other; the former adds a "dimension of wellness" to our being that is undeserved, even if needed to satisfy us, while the latter carves

out an empty "dimension of illness" within our being that bespeaks both a more-than-natural neediness and the possibility of a further undeserved gift of restoration. In such a view of the human being, there is no "neutral condition." We are in a condition of either well-being or ill-being; we are going either toward or away from God. One of Anselm's primary intentions in this chapter (and the various images and metaphors employed in it) is to illuminate this "intelligible structure" of human existence, this dynamic "in-between-ness" that we can identify as the "human condition." For it is in understanding these nested dimensions of our own human existence that we are able to arrive at insight into the ever-greater, yet self-contained dimension of divine existence.

19 Psalm 78:9.
20 In this opening chapter Anselm begins to capitalize on connections between the following words that share the same root *miser* ("pitiful"): *misere* ("pitifully"), *miserabiliter* ("pitiably"), *misericors* ("pity-hearted," traditionally rendered "merciful"), and *misericordia* ("pity-heartedness," traditionally rendered "mercy"). Some of my renderings go against convention, but taken altogether they convey better the connotations Anselm intends when using these words. Such renderings also bring to light other connections that Anselm utilizes later in Chapters 8–11.
21 Job 3:24.
22 Psalm 37:5.
23 Psalm 68:16.
24 Anselm articulates the image of God in us in way that points to our temporality: remembering is a connection to the past, thinking occurs in the present, and loving is aimed toward the future. This threefold temporal structure pervades the work and maps on to (among other things) the threefold task of the work itself as well as, of course, the Trinitarian God in whom Anselm believes and whom he is endeavoring to think.
25 Isaiah 7:9. In this last line of the opening chapter, Anselm indicates an interesting "meta-belief," i.e., believing that believing leads to understanding. He suggests, in other words, that trust underlies all human intellectual endeavors, especially the highest human intellectual endeavor, namely, the attempt to know the reality that grounds the intelligibility of all things. At both the beginning and the end of the human intellectual life, "faith seeking understanding" or "trust striving after insight" describes what is going on. We begin our intellectual lives, for example, by trusting others and the language we have learned from them, trusting the capacities we have (including our senses), trusting our experience, and the like, and on the basis of such trust we move toward basic understandings or insights. Moreover, we "end" or culminate our intellectual lives by trusting or assenting to a proposal of God (e.g., that God is "something than which nothing greater is able to be thought") and allowing that assent to lead us toward greater insights into God. At the beginning, then, we acquiesce to God the creator, i.e., we entrust ourselves to God as the giver of our nature and its cognitive capacities; whereas at the end we acquiesce to God the revealer, i.e., we entrust ourselves to his loving self-disclosure. Such underlying trust suggests that "intellectual hope" informs our cognitive encounters with reality and inclines us toward successful insights, both when we follow the impetus from God at the beginning of our intellectual lives and when

we accept a word from God at the end. Recognizing and taking seriously this "Anselmian epistemology" is important for seeing what he is up to in the remainder of the *Proslogion*, especially in Chapters 2–4.

26   In this chapter Anselm does not take up the claim that God is; rather, he takes up the claim that God *truly* is (*quod Deus vere est* [emphasis added]). From the Preface we know that Anselm is seeking first to build toward the fact that God truly is, i.e., the true manner, the manifestness, of God's existence. He does so by trying to capture the manifestness of God's existence in an act of speech that signifies human thinking that accords with the reality of God. The articulation of God as "something than which nothing greater is able to be thought" embodies Anselm's attempt to do this.

    This initial task of the *Proslogion* makes more sense when it is seen in light of the account of truth laid out by Anselm in his subsequent work *De veritate*, a dialogue between a teacher and his student who are trying to articulate a notion of truth applicable to both God and other things. After discussing the truth of speech acts, opinions, wills, actions, sense perceptions, and beings themselves, the teacher and student arrive at an account of truth as *rectitudo mente sola perceptibilis*, "rightness [or: straightness] able-to-be-perceived by the mind alone." According to this account, something is true inasmuch as it is "right" or "straight" in relation to its end or object, which is determined in created realities ultimately by God's intention in having made it as the sort of thing it is. Consequently, Anselm's first objective in the *Proslogion* – to build toward the fact that God truly is – consists in aligning his thinking with the reality of God, whose existence is true or manifest in the abovemost way. Carrying this out entails finding a precise and adequate way of signifying right thinking about the reality of God in speech. The "argument" that follows, then, is not so much "syllogistic" as "evidentiary." In other words, it attempts to unveil God as the ground or basis of the intelligibility of things, a ground first articulated as "something than which nothing greater is able to be thought." Anselm aims to show that once this divine ground is unveiled, one cannot think that it is not real, because it underlies the very activity of thinking as well as the very thinkability of the things we think.

27   The *ergo* ("therefore") in this opening line indicates continuity with what has just preceded. The original text of the *Proslogion* was continuous and indicated chapter divisions in the margins. To get a sense of the continuity of the original text, it helps to read the last three sentences of Chapter 1 and the first two sentences of Chapter 2 in a nonstop fashion; for this reveals how Anselm intends to carry out the activity of "faith seeking understanding" articulated at the end of Chapter 1 in relation to the proposed thought of God as "something than which nothing greater is able to be thought" at the beginning of Chapter 2. The reader is asked to acquiesce, to entrust, to give himself over to this thought in order to see where it leads; for it leads, Anselm thinks, to an insight into the necessary existence of God underlying the intelligibility of created reality.

28   At times I italicize forms of the verb "to be" in order to indicate when the Latin wording suggests a reference to being or existing as an activity in its own right (as opposed to a factical or copulative use of the verb "to be").

29 Psalm 13:1; 52:1. This Psalm, taken as a whole, suggests that in fact every human being is a "fool" (*insipiens*; more literally, "unwise"). As the Psalmist says, "The Lord looks down from heaven upon the children of men, to see if there are any that act wisely, that seek after God. They have all gone astray, they are all alike corrupt; there is none that does good, no, not one" (RSVCE). Undoubtedly, then, among the fools who do not act wisely, Anselm counts himself.

This verse from the Psalm also suggests that the question of God's existence is a question of the heart (*cor*), not simply the mind (*mens*) or the understanding (*intellectus*). If one considers the passages in which Anselm uses *cor* in the preceding chapter, it appears that by the "heart" Anselm understands the human being's existential center, the primal source of cognitivity and affectivity unique to every person. *Cor* is used five times in Chapter 1, and each use points to a different aspect of it. The heart can speak, be taught, groan, be embittered, and believe and love. And in this passage at the opening of Chapter 2, the heart is the place where the fool speaks his denial of God's existence – and, presumably, the place where the wise man affirms God's existence.

30 According to Anselm, by means of the original *cogitatio* (i.e., the activity of thinking something than which nothing greater is able to be thought), one comes to see both that this thought signifies a unique and necessary divine existence that underlies and creates all things, and that those things that it underlies are created inasmuch as they do not have such necessary existence. This connection becomes clearer especially in Anselm's Reply, [I].

31 The problem with the fool, then, is that he does not take the meaning of "something than which nothing greater is able to be thought" fully to heart. He hovers on the surface of its signification rather than giving himself over to its significative power. It is possible, then, for a human being to deny God's existence, but this is because human beings are capable of intellectual superficiality and thus can fail to see the ground for the very thinkability of the world in terms of its hierarchical structures.

32 Anselm introduces a methodological or operative principle for unfolding the intelligibility of God as something than which nothing greater is able to be thought, namely, that he is "whatever it is better to be than not to be." Hence we are subtly moved from God as *maius* ("greater") to God as *melius* ("better"), i.e., a move from a more "quantitative" consideration of God to one that is more "qualitative." Chapter 5, then, marks a turning-point in the work; it is transitional. In the subsequent chapters Anselm begins to articulate true aspects or "attributes" of the divine reality, based on the fact of God's creative causality. Hence, after the rousing of Chapter 1, Chapters 2–4 constitute a unified (tripartite) section of the *Proslogion*. Then, having achieved an understanding of the necessity of God's existence as the creator, our thinking God embarks on a different course in Chapter 5, and we navigate this course by means of the principle that God is "whatever it is better to be than not to be."

33 The feature in question here is *sensibilis*, but in this chapter Anselm obviously addresses the ability to sense, not the ability to be sensed. Hence I render it "capable of sensing." Regarding the ability to be sensed, Anselm appears to take this up in Chapter 17 when he considers that "in God there is harmony, odor, flavor,

softness, and beauty, each in its own inexpressible manner." Chapters 6 and 17, therefore, are complementary; each is the inverse of the other, i.e., the other "turned inside out."

34   Usually *omnipotens* is rendered "all-powerful," "almighty," or "omnipotent," I render it "all-able" in order to bring out connections Anselm makes between various words stemming from the verb *posse* ("to be able"), such as *potens* ("able"), *potentia* ("ability"), and *impotentia* ("inability"). These connections are significant especially in Chapter 7.

35   After presenting a divine reality beyond reach as something than which nothing greater is able to be thought, Anselm "lowers" his thinking of God by considering him as *sensibilis*, "capable of sensing," a feature tied up with being bodily. This "downward" thinking of God is complemented in the next chapter with "upward" thinking, i.e., God as *omnipotens* ("all-able"), a feature that seems to put God out of reach. Then in the subsequent chapter the tension one might experience between God as perceptively present to all things and God as able to do whatever he wants is eased by a consideration of God as *misericors* ("pity-hearted") and *impassibilis* ("incapable of suffering"). This movement in Anselm's thinking is "erotic" in character; it attempts to get at the whole of God by moving lower, then higher, and finally deeper in a step-by-step fashion – or, in the terms of Plato's *Symposium*, it is a movement of thinking that is first comic, then tragic, and finally philosophic. Anselm's unfolding of the intelligibility of something than which nothing greater is able to be thought in these chapters, then, is not random, as it may first appear; rather, he approaches God with the deliberate intention of being adequate in his thinking both to the "greaterness" of the God the creator and to created human cognitivity, i.e., the cognitivity of an "amphibious" intellectual creature whose capacity to think is tied up with the capacity to sense.

36   In addition to the pattern of "erotic" thinking that characterizes Anselm's movement from one divine attribute to another, there is also a pattern within the treatment of each attribute. Put most succinctly, this latter movement goes from affirmation to negation to super-affirmation, a pattern that aligns itself with the traditional three *viae* ("ways" or "paths") to God, namely, *via causalitatis* (the way of causality), *via remotionis* or *via negativa* (the way of removal or negation), and *via eminentiae* (the way of eminence). In Chapter 5 Anselm says that God is the maker of all things who is "whatever it is better to be than not to be." As the maker or cause of each way of being better, God himself somehow possesses that way of being better (*via causalitatis*). But according to the manner in which we understand that attribute in created realities, that way of being better is tied up with limitations that belong to created being as such, and thus one should deny that attribute of God or at least question it (*via remotionis*). Yet affirmation is always prior to negation, and we cannot forget God as the cause of that attribute. Hence the tension between the affirmation and negation of each attribute issues in a super-affirmation, i.e., a reaffirmation of the attribute in a manner that fits the unique abovemost character of something than which nothing greater is able to be thought (*via eminentiae*). One can discern this pattern in Chapter 6 with regard to God as *sensibilis* ("capable of sensing"), and a similar pattern emerges more or less explicitly in Anselm's treatment of each divine attribute.

37   Here Anselm brings to light a distinction that helps us think more clearly about
      God as *omnipotens* ("all-able"). In addition, his short explication provides a hint
      for understanding the manner of thinking God in which Anselm is engaged in this
      portion of the *Proslogion*. After arguing that what some things are able to do actu-
      ally manifests inability rather than genuine ability, Anselm suggests another way
      of considering *posse* ("to be able") that is similar to an improper "different kind
      of speaking" in which we sometimes engage when we use other basic verbs, such
      as *esse* ("to be") and *facere* ("to make" or "to do"). The examples to which Anselm
      points indicate how by the same word we easily refer to what are in fact polar
      opposites of each other. For instance, we often say "being" or "doing" with refer-
      ence to both the presence and absence of actual being or actual doing. The point
      Anselm wants to make is first a grammatical one, namely, that sometimes when
      we say that a subject "is able," we are actually signifying an inability that belongs
      to it. Hence in order to understand God as "all-able," we need to see that it includes
      only those "abilities" that name positive or real strengths in a being and not those
      that are in fact inabilities or creaturely weaknesses. This ability to "purify" signi-
      fications of their limited or even negative aspects so that they can be attributed fit-
      tingly to God is crucial for the super-affirmative moves Anselm makes in these
      chapters.
           Perhaps by introducing this improper way of speaking, Anselm also points to
      the mysterious ability of human thought to hover over being and nonbeing, doing
      and nondoing. This aspect of thinking, manifest in these grammatically improper
      (and yet acceptable and understandable) ways of speaking, suggest a divine-like
      stance toward being and nonbeing, i.e., the way in which speech gives "being" in
      thought to what is in fact nonbeing in reality. At the same time, however, this very
      ability of ours to speak improperly also indicates our weakness as intellectual
      creatures, insofar as much of our thinking is tied up with the being-and-nonbeing
      of creaturely existence and is not focused on the pure existence, the great "I am,"
      of the Creator.
38   Here the advantage of translating *misericors* as "pity-hearted" rather than "merci-
      ful" becomes evident, inasmuch as "pity-hearted" makes more apparent the ten-
      sion between thinking God as pitying, i.e., sensing or feeling something in
      response to our situation, on the one hand, and thinking him as *impassibilis*, "inca-
      pable of suffering," inasmuch as he does not sense or have feelings but is altogeth-
      er active in his all-ability (as is evident from the last line of Chapter 7). "Merciful"
      is too abstract a rendering of *misericors* to capture this tension well, which tension
      traces back to our thinking God as both *sensibilis* ("capable of sensing") and
      omnipotens ("all-able" in a purely active sense). The more literal renderings, then,
      portray better the difficulties Anselm is facing in the *Proslogion* when he tries to
      articulate true aspects of the divine existence in human terms.
39   According to our initial way of thinking, pity-heartedness (or mercy) and justice
      are opposed to one another; for in the former case one chooses not to give what is
      owed (namely, a punishment), whereas in the latter case one is bound to give what
      is owed. This tension between thinking God in a "lower" (i.e., more "bodily" or
      "sensible") way as pity-hearted and thinking God in a "higher" (i.e., more "spiri-
      tual" or "abstract") way as just is eventually resolved by thinking God in a

"deeper" way as *bonus* ("good"). For as we find out in what ensues, both divine pity-heartedness and divine justice flow from divine goodness.

40   I Tim. 6:16.

41   The image that Anselm employs here, i.e., that goodness is like a spring from which both pity-heartedness and justice flow, helps us begin to see God's exercise of mercy and justice not from a human perspective, from which we are prone to consider God as reactive or responsive to an already given situation, but from a deeper perspective, from which we consider God as actively – not reactively – manifesting his goodness as either mercy or justice, as he deems fit. Understanding this pure "activity" (and "non-reactivity") of God as creator is crucial for understanding the picture of God that comes into focus in these chapters. A culmination of sorts is reached when God is seen as good, as goodness itself, as the self-diffusive source of all else that is. From our perspective, then, we see and experience both mercy and justice; but from the divine perspective from which we are attempting to look, both are simply goodness manifesting itself as God wills. As we see near the end of Chapter 11, however, this "reduction" or "leading-back" of mercy and justice into goodness does not eliminate all tension in our thinking God. In fact, it may lead to greater tension, inasmuch as "it certainly is able to be comprehended by no reason why [God] save[s] these rather than those from like evils through the abovemost goodness and why [he] condemn[s] those rather than these through the abovemost justice."

42   A strange turn of events: God is pity-hearted because he is just! This is because pity-heartedness is "owed" or fitting to God inasmuch as he is good. Indeed, as Anselm says near the end of Chapter 10 just below, "Hence, by saving us whom you might justly destroy, just as you are pity-hearted not because you feel an effect, but because we feel an effect, so also you are just not because you render to us what is owed, but *because you do what is becoming to you as good in the abovemost way*" (emphasis added).

43   Psalm 24:10.

44   Psalm 144:17.

45   Psalm 24:10.

46   Psalm 144:17.

47   Here Anselm reaches a peak in his contemplation of God's pity-heartedness and justice. From this peak he sees that God himself is the ultimate standard; he is not subject to any higher standard. Such a claim does not mean that God is irrational, but that he is super-rational, i.e., that he stands beyond the reach of human understanding. As Anselm goes on to say, when we reach this peak, we realize that when it comes down to particular cases, we are unable to account fully for why God chooses to manifest his goodness in one case as justice and in another case as pity-heartedness. Indeed, to think that we could come up with such an account of God's activity in a particular case would entail, as Anselm says in Chapter 3, that "a creature would ascend above the Creator and would judge about the Creator – which is very absurd."

48   This "summary" of divine attributes suggests a conclusion of some sort. If so, it means that Chapters 6–11 (and perhaps including Chapter 12, which briefly considers divine "simplicity") constitute a unified section of the *Proslogion*. It may

also indicate that Chapters 13 and 14, which are the central chapters of the entire work, serve as a kind of turning-point in Anselm's thinking God. And on the "other side" of these chapters, in Chapter 15, Anselm in fact re-articulates his thought of God as "something greater than is able to be thought."

49 Psalm 42:3.
50 I John 3:2.
51 I John 1:5.
52 It would take us too far afield to distinguish fully between this new thought of God as "something greater than is able to be thought" and the initial thought of God as "something than which nothing greater is able to be thought" introduced in Chapter 2. But at least one likeness and one difference should be noted here. The thoughts are similar insofar as each is comparative in character. This is an important point, because for Anselm distinction-making and comparative thinking are crucial to exercising rationality. As he says in Chapter 68 of the *Monologion*, "[T]o be rational for a rational nature is nothing other than to be able to discern what is just from what is not just, what is true from what is not true, what is good from what is not good, and what is more good from what is less good." The thoughts are different, however, insofar as they compare different "things." The comparison in the initial thought is between the "divine something" and anything else that is able to be thought, whereas the comparison in this new thought is between the "divine something" and "thinkability" itself. To put this a bit differently, one could say that the initial thought compares thinkable objects to God as an "object" of thought, and it suggests that as a "thinkable object" God is ever-surpassing; whereas this new thought of God culminates that way of thinking God as an "object" by suggesting that he is not in fact an "object," but is actually beyond thinkability. Hence this second thought suggests that God is the very source of the thinkability of things – or, in other words, God is "light," the description of God that Anselm introduces in the subsequent chapter. In this way Anselm effects a subtle move in the text from thinking God transcendently to thinking God immanently.
53 I Tim. 6:16.
54 Acts 17:28.
55 Compare this sentence to what Anselm says above in Chapter 6: "Therefore, Lord, although you are not a body, yet truly you are capable of sensing in the abovemost way – in that manner in which you recognize all things in the abovemost way, not in the manner in which an animal recognizes something by a bodily sense." Combining these two assertions, we see that God is capable of sensing in the abovemost way and that he has all sensible qualities in an inexpressible way. Hence, with regard to both of the "flip" or complementary sides of the act of sensation (i.e., the side of the one sensing and the side of what is sensed), God stands as ultimate.

In light of the complementarity of the attributes of "capable of sensing" (Chapter 6) and having sensible qualities (Chapter 17), one might wonder whether the other attributes Anselm articulates should be paired together as "flip sides" of each other. If one were to follow through on this line of thinking and follow the order in which Anselm treats God attributes, they might be complementarily paired thus: all-able / having no parts; pity-hearted / having all places and times in himself; just / being what he is and who he is; and good / being Father, Son, and Spirit. (The last pairing Anselm himself suggests in the title of Chapter 23.) Although it would take us beyond the limits of these notes, it would be well worth our time to explore these pairings in order to see if and/or how they complement and illuminate each other.

56 Psalm 50:7.

57 Romans 5:12.

58 Psalm 24:7.

59 Psalm 26:8.

60 Psalm 12:4.

61 Psalm 89:2.

62 Luke 10:42.

63 The title of this chapter suggests a new manner of thinking, namely, *coniectatio* ("conjecturing"). To conjecture (*conicere*) is literally "to throw/cast together"; it is forward-looking, "projective" thinking. The title also indicates that Chapter 1 and Chapter 24 mirror each other, inasmuch as both chapters reenact a specific activity of thinking. Chapter 1 reenacts the rousing that precedes contemplation; Chapter 24 begins the conjecturing that succeeds contemplation. Indeed, the opening word of Chapter 24 – *Excita* ("Rouse") – suggests such a connection. Anselm begins the *Proslogion* by rousing us toward contemplating God; then, having contemplated God at length in Chapters 2–23, in Chapters 24–26 he conjectures or projects for us an afterlife in union with God. Thus Anselm concludes the *Proslogion* by endeavoring to depict the life to come in which we will (hopefully) be united to something than which nothing greater is able to be thought, who is likewise something greater than is able to be thought, the one thing necessary, who is every and the one and the whole and the only good.

64 This sentence introduces a third way of articulating or thinking God around which the *Proslogion* pivots, namely, God as "that [delightful] good . . . which contains the pleasantness of all goods." In all, then, Anselm presents us with three pivotal ways of thinking God: God as "something than which nothing greater is able to be thought" (Chapter 2); God as "something greater than is able to be thought" (Chapter 15); and God as "that [delightful] good . . . which contains the pleasantness of all goods." One could consider these thoughts of God as corresponding with the three activities by which Anselm defines us as images of God in Chapter 1, namely, thinking, remembering, and loving. In turn, these activities bespeak the present, past, and future dimensions of our temporal existence. And undoubtedly Anselm expects us to see these threefold structures as reflective of the Trinitarian divine source whom we human beings image.

65 The titles of Chapters 25 and 26 are in the form of questions, which suggests the open-endedness of the projective thinking with which Anselm concludes the *Proslogion*.

66 I Corinthians 2:9.

67 In these opening sentences of Chapter 25, Anselm distinguishes goods of the body from goods of the soul. The ensuing paragraph treats the goods of the body, while the paragraph after that treats the goods of the soul.

68 Matthew 13:43.

69 Matthew 22:30.
70 I Corinthians 15:44.
71 Wisdom 5:16; Psalm 36:39.
72 Psalm 16:15.
73 Psalm 35:9.
74 Psalm 35:9.
75 Matthew 25:21–23.
76 Matthew 5:9.
77 Romans 8:17.
78 Matthew 22:37.
79 John 16:24.
80 Matthew 25:21.
81 I Corinthians 2:9.
82 I Corinthians 2:9.
83 John 16:24.
84 John 16:24.
85 Matthew 25:21.
86 Romans 1:25.

Gaunilo's Objections

1 Augustine, *In Evangelium Joannis tractatus*, I.16 (PL 35, 1387).

Anselm's Reply

1 As Anselm indicates in the opening sentence of his reply, he is addressing Gaunilo as a *catholicus* ("Catholic Christian"). Hence he feels free to appeal to Gaunilo's "faith and conscience," which he does in this paragraph. His argument seems to run as follows: If to believe or to have faith is to think with assent, then God in some way has to be able to be thought or to be in understanding. For the Catholic Christian, moreover, God has to be that than which a greater is not able to be thought; otherwise, such a believer would have to say – absurdly, it seems – that he can think of something greater than God. As a Catholic Christian, then, Gaunilo must admit that that than which a greater is not able to be thought is able to be thought or is in understanding. Hence Gaunilo's real criticism should concern the *consequences* of its being able to be thought or to be in understanding, not the *fact* that it is thought or is in understanding. Indeed, near the beginning of Chapter 2 of the *Proslogion*, Anselm introduces this thought of God as something that is believed communally, presumably by Catholic Christians: "And indeed *we believe* that you are something than which nothing greater is able to be thought" (emphasis added).

It is worth noting, too, that later in his reply (in [VIII]) Anselm spells out a way of arriving at this thought of God by considering degrees of goodness in reality. This indicates a way that this thought of God can be conjectured from a contemplation of reality. Hence it does not necessarily have to be something believed in by a Catholic Christian through the gift of faith.

2 It is difficult to know how to take Anselm's *plus aliquid* ("something more") in

this paragraph. Unlike what he does in the previous paragraphs, it appears that he supplements his argument in Chapters 2–4 of the *Proslogion* by indicating the sort of thinking at work in the argument. He does this by introducing the notion of something being "sub-understood," which he appears to pull from Boethius's translation of Porphyry's *Isagoge*. In fact, he uses *cogitari* ("to be thought") and *subintelligi* ("to be sub-understood") interchangeably in the rest of the paragraph.

The verb *subintelligi*, which translates the Greek verb *epinoêthênai* used by Porphyry, shows up three times in Boethius's translation in the following passages:

(a) "Now, an accident [*accidens*] is that which is present-in or absent-from without destroying the subject. But it is divided into two: into the separable and the inseparable. For sleeping is a separable accident, while being black happens [*accidit*] to the crow and the Ethiopian inseparably. But both a white crow and an Ethiopian losing his color are able to be sub-understood [*subintelligi*] without destroying the subject" (V.1–3).

(b) "Further, indeed, genera are prior to the differences that are posited under them, on account of the fact that when one takes away the differences, the genus is not at once taken away; for when animal is taken away, rational and non-rational are taken away. But differences do not take away the genus; for if all the differences are done away with, still living sensitive substance – which an animal is – is able to be sub-understood [*subintelligi*]" (VIII.4).

(c) "And the species is able to be sub-understood [*subintelligi*] before the accidents, even if they are inseparable; for there has to be a subject in order that something happen to it [*accidat*]" (XXIV.3).

It would be too much in a note to comment in detail on these passages, but perhaps a few words on being "sub-understood" are in order here. On the one hand, it looks like something can be sub-understood when, by means of a sort of imaginative exercise, one recognizes the enduring presence of a subject despite the absence of a regular feature or inseparable accident. Hence even though such a bird has never been seen, a white crow is able to be sub-understood, inasmuch as one has an insight into the fact that being black does not enter into a crow's very substance or subjecthood. Passages (a) and (c) get at this point. Likewise, a genus is able to be sub-understood apart from differences that determine it, as passage (b) indicates. Being an animal (i.e., being a living sensitive substance) is able to be sub-understood apart from those differences (rational and non-rational) that determine the animals one encounters in one's experience. Sub-understanding, therefore, involves an insight into what lies at the core of something, prior to and even apart from the features or determinations that are added, and this insight is aided by the work of imagination, which can remove or add features or differences in an attempt to see what endures.

By using this rare verb *subintelligi* in this paragraph, Anselm attempts to translate this notion of being sub-understood to realities determined by temporal and spatial dimensions. Reflecting on the particular time and place in which a reality exists yields insight into its not having to be in any particular time and place. In other words, any reality existing in a particular time and place is able to be thought or sub-understood as not being at anytime or anywhere at all. On the flip side, something than which nothing greater is able to be thought is not found in a particular place and time and, consequently, is not able to be thought or sub-understood not to be. By means of these reflections, it appears that Anselm articulates a basic distinction among realities, namely, the distinction between, on the one hand, realities that have some sort of "location" or determination and thus are able to be sub-understood not to be and, on the other hand, that unique something than which nothing greater is able to be thought, which is not able to be thought or sub-understood not to be. Insight into this latter, necessary reality is had, then, both by thinking the possible nonbeing that underlies each temporal-spatial reality and by endeavoring to think the necessary existence of something than which nothing greater is able to be thought.

For a reality to be sub-understood, then, involves the exercise of imagination operating in a hypothetical mode coupled with insight into the "logical" or intelligible structure that lies beneath the temporal, spatial existence of the world. Anselm indicates in this portion of his reply to Gaunilo that this sort of meditative thinking is at work in the *Proslogion* as a whole and in the argument of Chapters 2–4 in particular.

3   It is helpful to compare this paragraph with the paragraph in [I] above in which Anselm introduces the verb *subintelligi* ("to be sub-understood"). In conjunction with that paragraph, the reader begins to see the importance of the verb *cogitari* ("to be thought") in Anselm's articulation of his thought of God in the *Proslogion*.

4   The Latin participle here is *conscendendo* ("by a gathering ascent"), from the verb *conscendere*, a rare verb that in a way captures the intellectual movement toward God in Chapters 2–4 of the *Proslogion*. A few words later Anselm uses another verb, *conicere* ("to conjecture"), which follows upon this gathering mental ascent. The first verb indicates a movement of the mind that is both unifying (*con*) and upward (*scendere*), and in this portion of the reply to Gaunilo, Anselm shows how such a movement toward something than which nothing greater is able to be thought takes place by reflecting on and scaling the hierarchy of goodness that permeates reality. A plant is better than a rock, a dog than a plant, a human being than a dog, and so forth. When one moves through reality and its degrees of "greatness" in this rational way, one disposes oneself to go upward and beyond such determinate ways of being greater toward something than which nothing greater is able to be thought. From this gathering mental ascent, therefore, one is able to conjecture or "to cast forth in a unifying way" (*con-iacere*) a reality that embraces within itself and yet transcends all the ways of being greater evident in our experience, e.g., in the comparison between the living and the non-living, between the sensing and the non-sensing, between the intellectual and the non-intellectual, between the eternal and the temporal, between the unchanging and the changing, and so on.

Anselm hopes, no doubt, that such human *conscendere* or "gathering mental ascent," which issues in a conjecturing of something than which nothing greater is able to be thought, is met by a divine *condescendere*, a divine "condescension," a reaching downward by God that allows the human being to fulfill the potential for understanding contained in a conjectural act of thinking rooted in the experience of degrees of "greatness" in reality.

5   Romans 1:20. Anselm's citation of this verse of the Bible indicates that he does

not consider his argument in the *Proslogion* to be an "ontological argument" as it is understood nowadays, namely, as an argument that is "*a priori*," i.e., that operates in the realm of concepts alone, and thereby arrives at God's existence. In fact, this entire paragraph points to the way in which the *Proslogion* argument is rooted in the rational experience of reality in terms of degrees of goodness – or, perhaps better, degrees of "greatness" – which is precisely what makes it possible for us to navigate reality and choose within it. For, as we noted previously, Anselm says the following concerning rationality in Chapter 68 of the *Monologion*: "[T]o be rational for a rational nature is nothing other than to be able to discern what is just from what is not just, what is true from what is not true, what is good from what is not good, and what is more good from what is less good." Striving to straighten up one's mind toward something than which nothing greater is able to be thought, therefore, constitutes the very fulfillment of our rationality.